"Starting with the powerful and devastating experience of murder in a community, the author thoroughly studies and reflects on community reactions and responses, and then creates this profoundly moving and informing piece of work.

"A book that is easily read and understood by busy people.....grounded in solid Old Testament theology but presented in a conversational manner.

"The original poems and the sermons included here challenge us to trust and be fed by the God in whom we believe.

"It is especially helpful that the Awareness Guide is included in the book!

"The Bibliography is wonderful!!"

Rev. Dr. BonnaSue
Director
Graduate Counseling Program
Eastern Mennonite University
Harrisonburg, Virginia

May 1999

CROSSROADS CHOICES: CONFRONTING CHAOS

CROSSROADS CHOICES

Confronting Chaos

Barbara J. Thrash

Kekova Press
Denver

Library of Congress Cataloging-in-Publication Data

Thrash, Barbara J.
Crossroads choices: confronting chaos/ Barbara J.Thrash. --1st ed.
p. cm.
Includes bibliographical references and subject index.
LCCN: 99-90377
ISBN: 0-9671482-0-0

1. Adjustment (Psychology)—Religious aspects—
Christianity. 2. Christian life. 3. Self-help techniques.
4. Theology, Practical. 5. Church work with disaster victims. I. Title.

BV4909.T47 1999   248.8'6
QB199-579

Published in the United States of America
by Kekova Press
Cover by Orbit Design

ACKNOWLEDGMENTS

I wish to acknowledge the people who have been part of this project before I even knew it was possible.

My husband, Michael, who first encouraged me to consider writing a book and then listened, discussed, and proofread many versions many times, and finally published my book in an amazing and overwhelming support of me and my stories.

My daughters, Debbie and Libby, who claim these principles are what I've always said and who have taught me the value and joy of honesty.

Dr. William Campbell, consultant and friend, who helped me find focus in piles of research material that fascinated me and kept reminding me that I had a story to tell. He interviewed me, read several versions of manuscript, and made suggestions that helped to clarify the crossroads.

My long-time friend, Margaret McDermott, in the midst of her own *Chaos*, read and considered my work and encouraged me in this project. I wish her healing and good life.

My colleagues in seminary and in ministry: we studied, discussed, and worked together, experiencing hours of wonderful memories and significant exegesis.

My professors at Colgate Rochester Divinity School, especially Dr. Werner Lemke, who opened the world of the Old Testament and enabled me to see promise and hope in those texts, and Dr. James Poling, whose work in the area of evil has been so helpful to me.

My editor, Dr. Patricia Dean, who chopped and clarified and asked many questions while telling me how important this work was.

And many other helpers: Louise Garrison, Rochester, NY, who collected newspaper articles from the Rochester Public Library; Police Chief David Dalton, who was willing to reflect on the Palmyra murders years after they occurred; my readers, Barby and Gary Hahn, Mary-Beth McCaw, Barbara Campbell, Marla Kauerz, Jay Rundell, Pat and Larry Campbell, Cathy Thrash, and Virginia Thrash.

DEDICATION

Finally, I wish to thank the people about whom these
stories are written. Although I acknowledge and honor
the ones who died, I wish to dedicate this book to those
who lived: the people of the Palmyra First United
Methodist Church and the Palmyra community; my
parents and my brothers; and the Ecklund family, Lori,
Doug, Troy, and Alyssa.

May you always believe
that you are children of God
and, therefore, choose life
so that you and your descendents
may truly live!

I call heaven and earth
to witness against you today
that I have set before you
life and death,
blessings and curses.

Choose life
so that you and your descendants
may live.

Deuteronomy 30:19 (NRSV)

CONTENTS

PROLOGUE

Do not fear, for I have redeemed you; I have called
you by name, you are mine. When you pass
through the waters, I will be with you; and through
the rivers, they shall not overwhelm you; when you
walk through fire, you shall not be burned, and the
flame shall not consume you. For I am the Lord
your God, your Savior. Because you are precious in
my sight, and honored...... and I love you.
(Isaiah 43:1b-3a, 4a NRSV, adapted)

Being claimed by God has become the core of my spirituality. Now I know that I am a child of God. But I didn't always know it—in fact, I didn't even know it was important and basic to my understanding of life.

I believe that God is real and is the essence of life itself. Being claimed by God, or being a child of God, means that I am loved in spite of what I do or what I have done and not because of my successes or failures. When I open to this love, I am choosing life rather than death in the very midst of my living. Being a child of God means that I trust life, or God, to teach me, to comfort me, to strengthen me—but not to protect me or to ensure my success or my good health.

God is the giver of grace and love—God who is life itself —full of beauty and meaning. God invites each one of us to travel the road of life, knowing and recognizing the evil that is always present. For me, evil is the temptation to take a different road that might be easier or might bring instant relief, quick enjoyment, or a fast track out of some of the difficulties we encounter on our road.

God does not have a complete plan already worked out for us. God's plan is the road that stretches out before us farther than our eye can see, full of possibility but not full of certainty. It is tempting to think that walking with God along the road of our life will be a guarantee of a good and happy life. But that is not so. There are difficult possibilities as well as joyous ones. Walking with God on this road means that we will be comforted in difficult times—we will not be overcome by the waters or the flames, as it says in Isaiah. We will walk, facing the unknown however it comes to us, knowing that we are loved. Along that road, life becomes deeply meaningful. Trusting the process of life is another way of understanding the idea of walking with God. We trust in God and trust in the possibility of new life even when what we once knew is destroyed.

My beliefs have grown out of my life experiences, my studies, and my worship experiences. I grew up in a family where being a child of God was not part of our family language. But from a very young age, for some inexplicable reason, I yearned to belong to God.

My search for belonging drew me to the church community. As a three-year-old, I tagged along to church and choir practice with my neighbors; as a student in grade school and high school, I was involved in youth programs and church camp; as a college student, I led a youth group. As an adult, I sang in church choirs and got involved in Bible Study where I began to question, and then recognize, the significant role women played in the Bible. This began to instill in me the desire to enter the ministry, even though all of my own ministers had been male. Finally, I attended seminary where I was challenged to find meaning in ways I had never expected.

Many seminary and graduate students complain that academic study is a stumbling block to faith. For me, it was just the opposite. The study, the sharing of faith stories, the challenge to reflect on my life from a new perspective gave me the tools I had long been seeking.

My seminary experience provided me with the courage to look back at my family of origin and my family by marriage. That experience also prepared me to address some of the circumstances of the families in the churches I served. Murder was one circumstance for which I was unprepared. The impetus to write this book came after several years of reflection on the double murder that took place in Palmyra, New York, while I served as pastor of the United Methodist Church there. Those murders were so horrible, and the community's response (including the church's response) so confusing to me, that that period of my ministry has been the focus of my reflections since I left Palmyra. In the intervening years, I have sought out contemporary stories of persons who survived horrible times; I read and listened for the words that other pastors were speaking to those in the midst of crisis and the adjustments needed in the days and months that followed. I needed to hear those words myself, and I wanted to speak them through my writing to people like the ones who had trusted me as their pastor.

The stories I relate here illustrate three ways of dealing with the chaos that typically follows a crisis event in life. In the past I have been critical of my performance and that of other people involved in the first two events that I describe. Now it is important for me to acknowledge that I understand each of these experiences as holy and precious. Through them and through my reflection on what I experienced and learned, I have come to know that I am a child of God.

I want you to know that you are also. This book is intended to challenge your understanding of God. It is also designed to challenge your understanding of evil. It is my hope that reflection on your own experiences will bring you to new faith and deeper trust, for it is in this faith and trust that we are strengthened and able to endure difficult times—to stay on the road with God toward healing and wholeness.

Barbara J. Thrash
Denver, Colorado

ONE

CROSSROADS CHOICES

There is meaning in our existence, and it is the responsibility of each of us to find that meaning. The process portrayed in the diagram on the next page shows the way. Meaning is found by staying on the road of life in order to integrate all of life's experiences, including the often difficult and painful aspects that follow a crisis.

There are particular events that occur along this road. Some of these are events so disruptive that, in looking back, we might describe our lives as being calm before them and in chaos afterwards. Everyone has had these times of crisis, most of us many times.

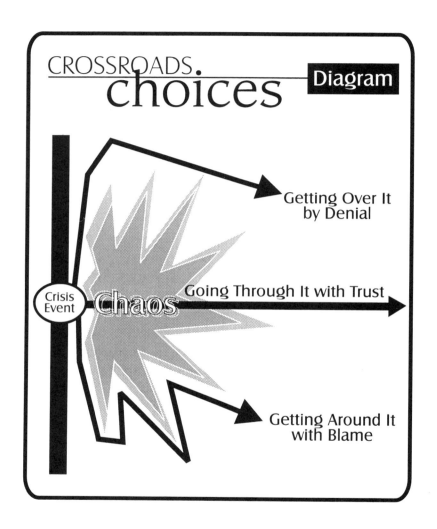

The focus in this book is the period of time after a Crisis Event. I have labeled this period of time *Chaos*, because it is unpredictable, disorienting, and varied. At first, the natural response is to try to carry on as we always have, to try to survive the shock. We are grateful for habits that seem to control themselves because we have done them so many times before— habits like brushing our teeth, doing the laundry, opening a can of soup, even eating.

Gradually, the initial shock and sense of confusion lifts. We may be so relieved that the confusion is gone that we might assume we are over the trauma of the crisis. Actually, we are in the midst of *Chaos,* and the process of dealing with that *Chaos* is just beginning. Until this time we have been in what is usually described as shock in response to the Crisis Event. We may feel as though we have been on a rough road that takes us forward a few steps, then backward, as our emotions push and pull us back and forth. Time is very distorted in *Chaos*. Some days it may seem as if the event just happened; there will be other days when it all seems to have been a bad dream. But the *Chaos* is not over, and it has not been completely processed. To assume that it is over would be a mistake.

3

<u>This is the *Crossroads*</u>. This is the time when we make a decision about how we will deal with the *Chaos* in the time ahead. The days of operating automatically were simply to get us started, to allow us to get to the place of making a choice. We may not be aware that we are choosing or even that we face a *Crossroads*. Our choice for dealing with *Chaos* is based on our family experiences, our observations of others dealing with the same kinds of crises, or on the conscious evaluation of our faith, our understanding of God, and the meaning of life itself.

It is possible to make a number of choices as we try to find a way through *Chaos*. We might try to hurry the process because it is too painful to experience. We might try to diminish the importance of the event or deny that it hurts so much. Or we might be overwhelmed by anger and try to find someone or something to blame.

No matter how many different choices we make at first, only one way will be the clear choice for the long term. That final choice is based on our true, underlying beliefs about life, about God, and about ourselves. Those beliefs are not necessarily the ones we proclaim aloud or even the ones we think we hold.

4

Some of our deepest beliefs are based on assumptions that we have not had the opportunity or occasion to examine. These beliefs are the basis of our understanding about life, and they affect the choices we make in every aspect of our lives, even those not related to *Chaos* or Crisis Events. These beliefs determine the words we say to our children in loving them, in disciplining them, in punishing them, or in teaching them.

Being a Child of God

Most importantly, your beliefs determine the words you say to express whether or not you know yourself to be a child of God. If you believe you are a child of God, you will recognize that Crisis Events are part of the totality of life. You will travel the road through *Chaos* integrating that experience into the wholeness of your life. You will trust that, difficult as it may be, you will make it through the experience all right. This trust comes from the basic belief that God is Good and Life is Good.

But you may be doubtful about your ability to deal with *Chaos,* and you will seek ways to get over or around it without having to experience it fully. The uncertainty that is part of *Chaos* will cause you to fear your feelings of loss or pain, and you will try to cover them up or make them go away. Essentially, you are unable to trust God or to trust the process of life and healing. You do not trust yourself to allow life itself to heal you. And you do not believe yourself to be a child of God.

The Importance of Choice

The way we choose to live through *Chaos* determines whether or not we will find deeper meaning for living the rest of our lives. Our choice at this *Crossroads* determines how we will face the next Crisis Event and the ensuing *Chaos* that happens in our life.

I believe that the goal for all of us is the healing of the suffering we experience in crisis—not merely the absence of pain. I also believe that every human being wants a good life. But there are times that we are so overwhelmed by our circumstances that we make choices that do not help us to achieve that goal. In this book I will discuss three choices that are commonly made in response to Crisis Events and *Chaos*, and I will show how one choice, *Going Through It*, helps to achieve the goal of healing so that we can trust life and experience it more fully.

It is my experience that the evaluation of our assumptions about God along with an examination of different ways to deal with *Chaos* will make healthy, holy choices more clear along the road of life. It will lessen the possibilities of taking one of the other roads that lead away from healing. The process of learning and examining your life will help you learn that you are indeed a child of God.

Getting Around It

The first choice you might make is *Getting Around It*. In this choice you want to find someone or something to blame for the event that has occurred along the way. If the event is particularly horrible, beyond your human understanding, you may choose to say, "Satan did it." If you are more oriented toward human responsibility, you may blame yourself or someone else. Any of these solutions suggest that you are determined to find the cause of the event that feels so wrong and is so difficult. *Getting Around It* by blaming will not

7

bring you to your goal of healing because your focus is actually outside yourself and on someone or something else. You have lost touch with the self, *you*, that needs healing, and you are unable to feel or experience the healing you most desire.

Getting Over It

The second choice you might make is *Getting Over It*. You may actually say, "I just need to get over it and get on with my life." This approach reveals that you choose not to integrate the Crisis Event into your life. In other words, you deny the importance of it in your life. *Getting Over It* suggests that the event does not belong in your life and that if you can just get over this unpleasant time, you can get on with your real life. It is as though life is only made up of pleasant, controlled moments; the rest can be rejected. This choice will not lead you to healing any more than the first. However, you may pretend that it does by outwardly denying your feelings or the impact of the Crisis Event on your life while inwardly protecting yourself from pain and the possibility of the next Crisis Event. Though you may pretend and try to convince yourself that you can control events so that nothing bad will happen, you are quite aware that bad things happen all the time. And you know they will probably happen in your life, because they have in the past. So you protect yourself in the only way you know how; you become frozen to real feelings and unable to experience the healing you most desire.

Going Through It

The third choice, *Going Through It*, is made by going through the middle of the *Chaos*. This means that you will fully experience life, with its deep sorrows and intense joys. When you make this choice, you are on the way to reaching the goal of healing that will lead to meaning in your life; but this way is not easy. On this road you are challenged to face the tragedies, the enemies, the losses. You not only face these experiences, but you embrace them as important and unique aspects of the life you are living.

PRINCIPLES OF CROSSROADS CHOICES

1. Life has meaning and life is chaotic.

2. We can choose how to face *Chaos*.

3. If you choose *Getting Around It*, you find reasons to blame someone or something for the event that has disrupted your life.

4. If you choose *Getting Over It,* you deny that this event is part of your life or you deny the importance of this event.

5. If you choose *Going Through It,* you go through the middle of the *Chaos* on the road of your life, trusting that you will find healing, trusting that this is the holy way to live your life.

6. The way to find meaning in life is to go through *Chaos*.

A Biblical Example

On Palm Sunday, Jesus entered Jerusalem with
friends and others who were waving palms and
cheering him on in celebration and welcome. The
following week did not go as the friends had
anticipated, but Jesus was not surprised. He
shared a dinner with his friends and tried to
explain what was ahead; though he asked them to
remain with him while he prayed, they fell asleep.

When he was nailed to a cross and left to die, some
of his friends left him, fearful that this might
happen to them. The ones who remained, who wept
and waited together, were the ones who first heard
the message of Easter morning. They chose not to
deny knowing Jesus, and they were filled with joy
and amazement for the new thing that God had
accomplished—the Resurrection of Jesus, the
Christ!

Nearly two thousand years later we continue to re-
enact the week Christians call Holy. There are
many people who want to capture the joy and
amazement experienced by those few on the first
Easter morning. They know of others who have had
that experience, and they think they will find it in
a church on Easter morning amid all the flowers

and brass instruments playing songs of joy and celebration.

But the Easter celebration doesn't make sense to them, because it has been separated from the experience of Jesus' death on a cross. The traditional ritual observance of the death and betrayal of Jesus is not attended by many people, even by those who are faithful churchgoers the rest of the year. But it is not possible to grasp the fullness of Easter apart from the dark and terrible event of the day we call Good Friday. There can be no resurrection without the crucifixion.

If we view this story from the perspective of the Crossroads Choices Diagram, then the death of Jesus is the Crisis Event, and the next few days are the *Chaos*. Some tried to avoid the reality and the pain of the Chaos by *Denying* any connection with Jesus or by *Blaming* the Romans or the Jews for his death. The ones who stayed experienced *Healing* on that first Easter morning.

The joy, the celebration of Easter is our goal, for that is what *Healing* brings to our lives. It is achieved by *Going Through the Chaos* that follows a Crisis Event.

12

Historical Background for the Stories

The three stories that follow are true. In all of these stories you will read about choices that were made to deal with the *Chaos* after Crisis Events and about the consequences of those choices.

The first occurred in Palmyra, a mid-sized town in upstate New York located coincidentally at the crossroads of State Highway 21, which runs north and south, and State Highway 31, which runs east and west. That crossroads city was the location of the *Crossroads* that produced this book: <u>A crossroads is an intersection of roads that lead in different directions</u>. Which way should you go? The *Chaos* experienced by the Palmyra community has challenged me to consider choices that are made to deal with the *Chaos* following life's tragedies.

The story of the double murder in Palmyra is told in detail drawn largely from the police report of the incident. The *Chaos* I describe that followed that tragedy is a combination of my memory of events, of notes I kept during that time, and of newspaper accounts from the year following the murders. I was involved in that *Chaos*; I may have even contributed to it! It has taken years for me to begin to sort out what was so troubling to me.

13

My mother told me the second story several years ago when I asked for more information about my infant brother Gary, who died when I was young. I was surprised about how much detail she remembered. She told me that it was the worst time of her life; I am sure it was—and still is.

The third story is about a family I knew in Palmyra whose lives were disrupted by events that coincide in time with the murders I relate. As I thought back on the days I spent with Tracy, the child who was terminally ill, and members of her family, I wondered if I was idealizing them and their experiences during that time. Then I found the funeral service I had conducted for Tracy, with a list of all of the family members I met over those months, the names of the doctors and nurses and therapists that I met as they cared for Tracy, and the names of friends and neighbors who visited. I read the words I had written about it as it happened. I still believe they were, and are, special people.

The people in these stories are ordinary people. They are mostly good, well-intentioned people. Some made choices that diminished their lives, while others made choices that made their lives more complete.

The final section of the book is a discussion of the choices that were made at the *Crossroads* in each of the stories and the consequences of those choices. I believe both God and Satan, good and evil, were involved in those choices, and I include a discussion of my beliefs with an historical perspective.

The Epilogue, *Feed the People*, is the sermon that I preached in Palmyra on Sunday, August 5, 1990, four days after the murders. The congregation was a combination of American Baptists, Presbyterians, and United Methodists, as was our summer practice at that time. It was my turn to preach as we gathered in the Baptist church sanctuary. We celebrated Communion together and tried to begin the process of dealing with the *Chaos* surrounding us.

You, the reader, are invited to enter into these stories of real life and to remember your own experiences that are brought to mind as you read. The Guide to Awareness will assist you as an individual or as part of a group, asking questions related to each principle of Crossroads Choices and suggesting related material for further study or investigation. May you be blessed by the memories of your past and the promise and hope in your future!

TWO

GETTING AROUND IT
BLAMING

What Happened in Palmyra

When he was only sixteen, Chad Campbell was sentenced to eighteen years to life imprisonment for the murders of fifteen-year-old Cynthia "Cindy" Lewis and seventeen-month-old Curtis Rizzo, which had taken place eighteen months before. This is the account of what happened.

Nancy Lewis, Cindy's mother, called the police about 8:15 PM on Wednesday, August 1, 1990, to report that her daughter Cindy, who had been babysitting with Curtis Rizzo, had not returned home by 6:00 PM as expected. Carol Hartnagel,

Curtis' mother, reported that Curtis was also missing. When Hartnagel had returned from work, Curtis and Cindy were not in the house and the baby stroller was missing. She had assumed that Cindy had taken Curtis for a walk, as she often did. But when it started to get dark, the mothers, who were next-door neighbors, decided something was wrong.

The police began a search, interviewing neighbors along Stafford Street where Cindy and Curtis lived. The two families produced a flyer about the missing children. They had plenty of help distributing it.

Chad Campbell, who lived in the neighborhood, seemed particularly eager to help. Chad had been a school friend of Cindy, and some of her friends said they had dated for a while. The secretary at the Palmyra-Macedon Middle/High School (Pal-Mac), where Chad was working for the summer, reported that when Chad got to work at 7:00 AM Thursday, August 2, he seemed quite upset that Cindy and Curtis were still missing. He asked the secretary to go with him to the baseball fields behind the school to look for them. She declined. Later that day, Chad called Hartnagel to ask if he and his friends could ride their bikes on the trails behind Pal-Mac to see if they could find anything that the state police helicopter may have missed. Hartnagel wondered why he had asked for permission.

The throbbing sound of a helicopter circling overhead all day was a constant reminder to the townspeople that Cindy and Curtis still had not been found. Friends of the families speculated that Curtis' father, no longer in the home, had kidnapped them both. Neighbors tried to remember when they had seen Cindy or Curtis last. Even strangers were talking about the missing children as if they knew the families well. By mid-afternoon a small crowd had gathered at the town hall, wanting to hear news firsthand whenever the police had something to report. Chad Campbell was in the crowd.

When the news finally came, the cries of the parents could be heard throughout the halls of the courthouse. Everyone knew they had been given information about their children; it didn't take long for the news to spread.

The police report described what had been found:

"The body of Cynthia Lewis was located lying on her back approximately 200 feet south of the south edge

of the athletic field. Lewis was fully clothed with her shirt pulled up over her intact brassier[sic]. Lewis had multiple stab wounds to her face and body, her throat appeared to be cut from her left ear to her right ear. The infant, Curtis Rizzo, was located the same distance from the south edge of the athletic field and was about 3 feet northwest of the body of Cynthia Lewis. His head was facing east-southeast and the legs were west-northwest. The child was wearing a one-piece jumper and diaper. Rizzo had a large cut from his left ear across his throat." (Item 30, New York State Police Report)

When the announcement was made to the crowd gathered outside the town hall, some screamed, some cried, and some expressed confusion at how anything like this could have happened in Palmyra. Some were shocked that it could happen to someone they knew, or that it could happen to anyone at all. Chad Campbell was one of the ones who cried.

Palmyra residents began to ask one another who could have done such a thing in this quiet town located at a distance from the city. The streets of Palmyra were especially quiet that night. No children were allowed outside, and some slept in the closet or under their beds.

At 12:15 AM, Friday, in the early morning darkness, the Investigation Team met to review the statements they had collected. According to the Police Report, "several major flaws" were detected in the statements from Chad Campbell when compared to statements from other witnesses. The team decided to re-interview Chad immediately.

Two investigators spoke to Chad's parents in their home, informing them that their son was a strong suspect in the murders. The Campbells were advised of their rights—Chad's constitutional rights to have his parents or a lawyer present during questioning and their parental rights to be present during the interview. According to the police report, "all parties waived their rights" and, with parental consent, the police took Chad to the state police station for further questioning.

Only twenty minutes after being awakened at his home in Palmyra and rushed to the state police station thirty miles away in Newark, New York, Chad Campbell was "again advised of his rights under Miranda and again waived his rights." The police report indicates that "after a brief period of questioning Chad Campbell admitted killing both Cynthia Lewis and Curtis Rizzo with a fishing knife."

21

His confession reads as follows:

"He [Chad] advised he had telephoned [Cindy] Lewis at about 1:30 PM on [August 1, 1990], at the Lewis residence and requested Lewis meet him at the Palmyra Middle School [Pal-Mac] playground. Lewis agreed to meet him and about 10 minutes later did so. Campbell advised that she had the child Curtis Rizzo with her, in a stroller. He stated they talked and walked together toward the weeds behind the baseball field. Campbell stated he asked to hold Rizzo and after holding him a short time put him on the ground. Campbell then stated he reached into his rear pocket, pulled out his fishing knife and stabbed Cynthia Lewis several times in the chest. Lewis fell to the ground and Campbell stated he went to Rizzo and stabbed him in the throat. Campbell stated then the last thing he remembers of the incident, was pushing the stroller into the weeds and trying to hide it. Campbell then went back to his bike and threw the knife into the weeds. Campbell then rode his bike home, changed his clothes, went to [his aunt's] house and then to a soccer game in Macedon. Campbell stated he was alone when he committed these acts and that he had not told anyone about it. Campbell also drew a map of the area where the homicide took place and

indicated approximately where he had thrown the knife."

Soon after the confession was taken, at 3:55 AM on August 3, Chad Campbell was arraigned before Lyons Town Justice Nicholas Forgione on two counts of second-degree murder. He was committed to the Wayne County jail without bail and subsequently transported to the Monroe County juvenile detention facility in Rochester.

At 5:00 AM, just before dawn, Chad's parents were escorted back to their residence, where they produced the clothing allegedly worn by Campbell at the time of the murder.

At approximately 11:00 AM that day police found the knife where Campbell indicated he had thrown it.

At 5:30 PM the following day, August 4, using a search warrant obtained from Wayne County Court Judge Maurice Strobridge, police seized Campbell's bicycle from his residence.

On August 7, the Wayne County Grand Jury examined the cases against Chad Campbell and indicted him on two counts of second-degree murder.

On Wednesday, August 8, one week after the murders, Chad Campbell pled not guilty.

Slightly more than one year after the murders, on September 21, 1991, the trial of Chad Campbell began in the Wayne County courtroom in Newark, New York. Only seven days later, on September 28, the jury found him guilty of the murders of Cynthia Lewis and Curtis Rizzo.

On February 19, 1992, the Honorable Maurice E. Strobridge, Circuit Court Judge, Wayne County, sentenced Chad Campbell to nine years to life imprisonment for each murder, the terms to run consecutively, eighteen years to life.

Chaos in the Community

Two months after the murders of Cindy Lewis and Curtis Rizzo, Michael Hutchinson, age eighteen and a student at Pal-Mac, was found dead near the canal in Macedon, a small community a few miles west of Palmyra. His death, reportedly caused by an overdose of antihistamines, was ruled a suicide. His journal, which was found with him, indicated that he believed Chad Campbell had murdered Cindy and Curtis. When his death was announced at Pal-Mac, some students cheered, expressing a common suspicion that Michael had been involved in Satanism with Chad, perhaps even had been the leader of a cult. However, the police had interviewed Michael, and they did not consider him a suspect or connected in any way to the murders.

After Chad Campbell was arrested for murder in Palmyra, rumors about Satanism and satanic rituals traveled quickly. In preparation for his trial and defense, Chad's attorney, James Foley, made frequent and extensive use of the Satanism theory. In press releases to newspapers across several counties and in lecture-style reports with diagrams and flipcharts on the television evening news, he insisted that the police were dismissing the ritualistic significance of a grouping of rocks, found near the murder site, that Foley saw as evidence of Satanism. Foley was believed to be the source of a rumor that the deaths could be construed as a satanic ritual death of a virgin and child. He claimed that the date was significant: August 1 of every year is Laghnasdh or Grand Sabbat, one of the four great feast days in witchcraft and

Satanism. Finally, he contended that Michael Hutchinson had directed Chad to commit the murders.

In the confusion of those first days it was difficult to sort out truth from rumor. Besides, no one knew how to respond to the rumors. At first people simply tried to take care of the immediate needs of the families involved and to deal with their own family fears, rather than think about what the rumors suggested or what might happen if the rumors got out of control.

One might say they were at a *Crossroads*, responding to a crisis that no one had imagined could happen in this small town. Like others confronting tragedy, they sought an explanation for evil. What was its source? Was it Satan acting through certain young people? Was it rejected sexual desire converted into violence by a teenage boy, as suggested to me by a psychologist who studied the case? Was it drugs or alcohol, or families too busy to love and care for their children? Was it a spiritual emptiness in the community that was not responding to the needs of young people? Or was it spiritual questions of adults who seemed unable or unwilling to address any of these issues?

Although community leaders, clergy, school administrators, counselors, and the police had met several times to try to address some of the problems they believed people were facing, the biggest problem continued to be the constant rumors about satanic activity and the consequent potential for panic and hysteria.

It soon became clear that the one thing that could be done, in response to requests particularly from parents and teachers, was to organize a town meeting to address the issue of Satanism directly. The response to that meeting was overwhelming, while everything else that had been offered had been lukewarmly received. Over 1200 people crowded into the Pal-Mac auditorium; extra chairs were set up in separate rooms with satellite television feeds. Many people were turned away because there was no space inside or out. Tension was high, but there seemed to be a sense that finally there would be answers to the concerns surrounding the murders.

Jack Robinson, an investigator for the Wayne County Sheriff's Department; Robert Phenes, an investigator for the New York State Police; and local police chief David Dalton reported their findings. They assured the audience that they had found absolutely no evidence of Satanism at the murder scene. When asked if they had found rocks or sticks that appeared to have been set up in a pattern that would suggest satanic ritual, they said no. They asserted that they had taken seriously every call they had received about possible satanic activity, thoroughly investigating each one, and they urged people to continue to call in their concerns.

Chief Dalton added, tongue-in-cheek, that what some people had reported hearing in the cemetery at night was most likely the police who, as part of their investigation, had dressed in black and hidden in the bushes to check out possible satanic meetings or rituals. He reported that none had been observed. No one laughed at his attempted humor.

Wayne County Sheriff Richard Pisciotti showed slides of satanic graffiti and distributed handouts on satanic symbols and their meaning. He informed the audience that Satanism is not illegal. He described it as a devil-worshipping religion that is self-centered and self-gratifying to the participant. Noting that involvement in Satanism can range from simple curiosity to criminal involvement, he said that research at the criminal level had reached no conclusions as to whether persons already prone to violent crime are using Satanism as an excuse or whether their interest in Satanism came first. His information seemed to be exactly what many in the audience wanted to hear, since they already believed Satanism was active in Palmyra.

In response to further questioning, the local police admitted that police records from 1986 indicated that a monkey paw had been found in the middle of a road in town. At the time there had been some suspicion that it might have been related to a satanic sacrifice, but no further evidence was found. The police also acknowledged that they had recently seen satanic graffiti around the main cemetery.

Responding to the growing panic in the auditorium, Chief Dalton urged everyone to put things in perspective. The most important thing, he said, is to get kids off drugs and alcohol, because these create a vulnerability to Satanism. He assured the audience that the result of that specific intervention would greatly reduce the excessive interest in Satanism among teenagers. He also urged everyone to take teenagers' questions and concerns seriously, because they were searching for answers about life itself. He declared that many of them were "spiritually bankrupt," that they seemed to have no spiritual direction or understanding.

Finally, he proposed that a "rumor control board" be established, made up of clergy, law enforcement officers, and any others willing to help. The audience offered no response to the police chief's proposal or to his comments about teenagers.

Mark Head, a psychologist from Rochester who had worked extensively with families of teenagers involved in Satanism, directed his report specifically to families. Echoing Chief Dalton's suggestion that these teens might be "spiritually bankrupt," he asserted that Satanism feeds on the person's sense of spirituality, which may be a lack of spiritual understanding rather than something they believe deeply.

Teenagers, in general, feel powerless, he said, but some are especially attracted to the illusion of power they get when they express interest in a topic upsetting to the adults around them. Some of them are also critical of their parents' religion, especially what they interpret as its hypocrisy. "Religious people never do what they say others should, and they judge other people and not themselves," they say. A significant number of them come from rigid religious families, either "born again" Protestant or Roman Catholic. Head added that some of these teenagers seemed to be hopeless and pessimistic and to have given up on life.

"We do not have an epidemic of Satanism in our youth subculture either in Palmyra or in our country," Mr. Head said in conclusion. The police agreed, adding that Satanism is a limited phenomenon. A lot more has to be wrong first, they said, for people to be endangered by it.

By the end of the three-hour meeting, many frustrations and fears had been publicly expressed, but the worries about Satanism had not been contained or lessened. In response to requests, the police agreed to cover the old foundation at the cemetery, where many believed satanic ceremonies were being held, and to paint over satanic graffiti. However, the anticipated calming effect of the meeting had not been realized.

A year passed between the town meeting and the beginning of the trial of Chad Campbell. The continuous stream of information fed to the media by Chad's defense attorney stirred up rumors and fears all year long. School officials knew that the trial would heighten the rumors even more when students who were friends and acquaintances of Chad and Cindy were called to testify.

Summary

Referring to the Crossroads Choices Diagram on page 2, the Crisis Event in this story is the double murder. The *Chaos* was all that followed: the arrest of Chad Campbell, the suicide of Michael Hutchinson, the confusion and the questions and the rumors about Satanism. The response to the *Chaos* included the efforts of the community leaders to provide opportunities to discuss and consider everything that was happening.

This community, confronting this particular *Crossroads*, chose the option of *Getting Around It* by looking for something to blame for the murders that disrupted their community. Of course, blaming Satan was not the only choice made in the community, but it was the loudest and the most apparent choice.

The choice to blame Satan, an unidentifiable cosmic enemy, prevented the community from taking any steps toward addressing some of the problems presented by the murders. It prevented them from considering any other possible reasons for the murders; whether there might have been sexual, social, or theological reasons, or a combination.

The people in the community of Palmyra as a group did not believe, nor did they discover, that they were children of God in this experience, because they did not trust the process of healing. They were unable to wait in the uncertainty of not knowing what had happened or what could be done or why it happened—it was simply too uncomfortable for many different reasons. They rushed to find blame, to answer all the questions, before time and trust and faith could bring wisdom and understanding. That impatience pulled them away from the road toward healing.

Trusting in the process of life is trusting in God. This trust is experienced as patience in the midst of uncertainty and is based on the knowledge, the deep belief, that healing will come out of the most difficult experiences if we consciously choose not to place blame. This trust is experienced in our relationships between one another, and it is the basis of strong community. This trust was not experienced in Palmyra as the townspeople attempted to deal with the *Chaos* started by the murders.

33

THREE

GETTING OVER IT
DENYING

What Happened in My Family

In 1949 I was seven years old. I didn't know I
was a child, much less a child of God. I had big
responsibilities. It was my job to take care of
my three younger brothers, the oldest not yet five
and the youngest only nine months.

My mother was a young woman, not quite thirty
years old. That spring in early March, she had four
children and a husband who was suddenly
seriously ill. My father had been hospitalized and
was in an oxygen tent, probably suffering from
asthma and the beginnings of emphysema. I didn't
know until recently that my mother was afraid he

would die. She had wanted to be with him in the hospital, but she had small children who couldn't go inside, and she was still nursing the baby. On at least one of those March days, cold and rainy, she took the four of us with her to the hospital but left us in the car in the parking lot. I watched over the boys, and she came out when it was time to feed the baby.

That particular day was memorable to my mother because she believes that the baby, Gary, caught a cold. A few days later his breathing became quite labored and the doctor, who was on-call for our regular family doctor, said an emergency tracheotomy was necessary.

When I came home from school later that day, my parents were in the living room crying; my other two brothers were playing on the floor with trucks. I was eager to tell them I had found the coin purse I thought I had lost, but they didn't stop crying. They told me then that Gary had died.

I remember later that night Mom was hugging me so hard I thought I couldn't breathe. She was sobbing, and I thought then I would never be able to make her happy again. I wished that I had been the one who died; I was afraid she thought that, too. We didn't have a funeral, and for years we didn't talk about him or even say his name.

Many years later, in recognition of their fifty years of marriage, my parents prepared a collection of slides and pictures they had taken of family events over those years. It was quite a project for them; my father had been our photographer and had taken hundreds of pictures, and my mother had kept a scrapbook for each one of us. They had a large closet full of memorabilia, but I know they enjoyed sorting through all those years of memories.

One evening of the family gathering for the anniversary celebration, my parents showed the pictures as slides projected on the wall and reminisced about family events. Gary was part of that celebration in a series of pictures, and they spoke of him briefly. After the weekend, I rode to the airport with my youngest brother, born several years after Gary died, who was thirty-five years old at the time of the celebration. He said, "That is the most I have ever heard about Gary. I've always wondered about him because there are pictures of him in the scrapbook Mom kept of me."

Our family didn't talk about Gary's death. It was the most we could do just to get on with life. My parents worked hard to prevent losing any of the rest of us, focusing on our physical well-being.

A few years ago, when I asked my parents about Gary's death, I learned how sick my father had been at the time. Though I heard no sadness or even remorse in her voice as she spoke, I learned then that my mother had always believed Gary's death had been her fault. She had separated herself from the emotional impact of the event by forcing herself to move on so that she could take care of the rest of her children. Nevertheless, I felt an immense sense of loss as she talked—loss of the infant who was my brother, loss of my own childhood, and loss of my parents' sense of joy in their children. There was also loss of an important relationship, for we have grown steadily apart in the years since that event.

After that conversation with my parents, I planned a funeral service for Gary to celebrate his life, short as it was, forty-three years after his death. Part of that service follows.

Prayers for the Family

Holy God, whose ways are not our ways, and whose thoughts are not our thoughts, grant that your Holy Spirit may intercede for us with sighs too deep for our words. Heal the wounded hearts made heavy by years of sorrow that we have not acknowledged. Through the veil of our tears and the silence of our emptiness, assure us that ear has not heard, nor eye seen, nor human imagination envisioned what you have prepared for those who love you.

We are sure that neither death, nor life, nor angels, nor principalities, nor things present, nor things to come, nor powers, nor height, nor depth, nor anything else in all creation, will be able to separate us from the love of God in Christ Jesus our Lord.

Merciful God, we thank you for your word; it is a lamp for our feet, a light for our path. We thank you especially that in the night of our grief and in the shadows of our sorrow, we have not been left to ourselves. Though many years have passed since Gary's death, and we have failed as his family to honor his brief life with us, we know that you have valued the treasure of his life on earth, and that you continue to hold him within your eternity.

The pain of the loss of his presence with us is hidden in the folds of our hearts, and our unexpressed grief has hurt us in ways we do not understand. The loss of a child is a grievous burden. The guilt carried for years in mother and sister who cared for him have lessened the celebration of the lives that continued—life that you intended to be healthy and joyful and challenging.

May we, in these prayers of thanksgiving for Gary's life, also pray for ourselves, that we may finally release him to your keeping, knowing that nothing separates us in your love. We know that he is safe, and so are we, in your gracious love.

We ask that your gentle healing spirit may work within us, to heal the long untended wounds that have been covered over and ignored. We ask that the pain of the loss of brother and son may be healed, and that we may be set free from the bondage of guilt and grief.

With faith in your great mercy, O God, we entrust Gary to your eternal care. We acknowledge the unknown of eternity that binds us with all who have gone before us and all who are yet to come. Amen.

Summary

Referring to the Crossroads Choices Diagram on page 2, the Crisis Event in this story is the death of my brother. The *Chaos* was living with the loss and the silence, grieving in isolation, unresolved feelings, and confusion about death. The choice of my family at this *Crossroads* was *Getting Over It*, which led to denial. Consequently, we were unable to resolve the confusion and sense of loss, and we were unable to build trust between one another.

Denial separates the person from the event by an unspoken understanding that the event is not part of real life. It is as though the event as well as the person has been forgotten by not speaking the name; in fact, the effort is to forget, or at least diminish, the pain of the loss. It creates the impression that the *Chaos* is over and is no longer a concern. It may appear outwardly that the pain and suffering is over, but one consequence of denial is the inward effort to develop protection from hurt and loss in the pretense that feelings can be prevented, or at least controlled. The fear that grows internally begins to build a wall around the heart, a wall of protection that also keeps out experiences of joy and intimacy.

My family blocked out the loss and pain so effectively that we could not support one another. Because we could not trust this life experience, the experience of pain and sorrow in response to loss, none of us learned through this experience that we are children of God.

FOUR

GOING THROUGH IT TRUSTING

What Happened in Tracy's Family

Tracy's family came into my life not as members of my church, but through Tracy's grandmother. When three-year-old Tracy was diagnosed with brain cancer, her grandmother knew that her daughter's family was going to need some support in the months ahead. The family had been attending church in a nearby town, and the ministers there had encouraged them to find a church closer to their home to get the kind of help they were going to need. That was all Tracy's father, Doug, needed to hear. He was sure they could manage just fine without a church.

It was Doug I talked to the first few times I called, and I could hear his disinterest. Then I reached Tracy's mother, Lori. She was very much interested in visiting with me. In the months that followed, Lori and I had many theological conversations, shed many tears together, and shared our sense of frustration and anger. Together we prayed for insight and courage, sometimes just for strength to keep on waiting and hoping and loving Tracy.

Tracy had been diagnosed with brain cancer the year before and had already had a number of chemotherapy treatments. The prognosis was not good, and she was facing a serious neurological operation. An outstanding young surgeon at Johns Hopkins University Hospital had agreed to perform the operation. We had time, before the operation, to get acquainted and to talk about what they would face on that trip. I was impressed by their optimism. Tracy came through the surgery very well—she even told the nurses she didn't have a headache and didn't need any medicine when she was in the recovery room.

The next Sunday they were in church, and Tracy made her way to the front for the children's story. Lori chose to let her go on her own, and everyone watched Tracy's slow, slightly unbalanced steps and saw her big smile.

Following the surgery the doctor had told them that he had not removed the entire tumor because it was too embedded in the brain stem. He left it to them to decide what to do: completely removing the tumor would save Tracy's life but would mean that she would be bedridden for however long she might live; not doing further surgery meant that she would die fairly soon. After thinking about their lives, about Tracy's life and how much they loved her, and about their son Troy, an energetic, healthy five-year-old, Lori and Doug chose not to put Tracy through more surgery and to make the most of the time they had left with her. But they did decide she should have a bone marrow transplant in hopes it would make a difference in the way she felt and give them more time together.

By this time there were many people involved in their lives—church people, doctors, nurses, therapists, neighbors, friends, and a fairly large blended family who lived out of town but managed to visit often. After the bone marrow transplant, Tracy was able to get around a little on her own and to receive her many visitors.

Suddenly, and against all hope, Tracy went into a coma. Lori and Doug opted to keep her at home, doing their best to make life as normal as possible both for Tracy and for Troy. Doug went to work every day and spent evenings and weekends immersed in his family. Lori baked cookies and fixed meals, and Troy had friends over who ran around and made noise like most children do.

Troy frequently went in to Tracy to give her a picture or a kiss, or just to check on her. Lori and Doug were open with Troy about Tracy's illness. They prepared him for her death, often talking about how Tracy was going to be with God and sometimes praying with him. One day Lori told him that soon Tracy would go to be with God, so God could make her better and she wouldn't be sick anymore. Troy said, "Well, if God's going to make her better, then she can stay here. I want her to play with me!"

Lori cared for Tracy's physical needs with a gentleness that I had never seen. I watched her dress Tracy, place soft pillows under her arms, and hold her when she was restless. Once I watched her bathe Tracy and massage her with oil to keep her skin soft; it was an anointing as holy as any baptism I have ever witnessed. Lori's gentle,

46

unselfish manner, her loving of Tracy, was anointing me just by being there. It was so holy— and so wholly alive.

The amazing thing to me was Lori's ability to share her child with other people. The people who visited from the church, the nurses, the therapists, and friends and neighbors were all drawn to this family and to Tracy. Lori was open to receiving their concern and their care as they brought meals or presents or words of comfort, but she was also open to allowing them to hold and relate to Tracy however they chose.

Tracy died in the middle of the night in a friend's arms. That was very troubling to the friend, who thought she should have been with her mother, but even that was made all right by Lori's understanding. Because there was never any doubt that Lori loved and treasured Tracy, she was able to let Tracy be God's child, and not just hers. She truly believed that Tracy's life had been enriched by all the people who touched her and loved her.

Tracy's funeral was a celebration of her very short, but very lovely, life. It was a mixture of sadness and joy. It is always difficult to see the casket of a child. But many children came to the funeral (this was a family involved with many other families), and children bring noise and laughter, even to funerals.

The day of Tracy's funeral, several children drew pictures and placed them in her casket. Troy decided to give her one of his matchbox trucks. On the way to the cemetery Tracy's death became real for Troy when he realized he wasn't going to get his truck back. In the midst of both smiles and tears, his parents assured him they would get him another truck. What a gift they gave him in allowing him to be right where he was in his questions, his joy, and his grief.

Lori and Doug have since had another child, a girl they named Allyssa. Allyssa knows about Tracy and knows that she is her sister; in fact, she tells anyone who asks about their family that she has a sister who is in heaven. All of them, Lori, Doug, Troy, and Allyssa, know they are children of God.

From the Funeral Service
March 10, 1991

Immediately Jesus made the disciples get into the boat and go on ahead to other side, while he dismissed the crowds. And after he had dismissed the crowds, he went up the mountain by himself to pray. When evening came, he was there alone, but by this time the boat, battered by the waves, was far from the land, for the wind was against them. And early in the morning he came walking toward them on the sea. But when the disciples saw him walking on the sea, they were terrified, saying, "It is a ghost!" And they cried out in fear. But immediately, Jesus spoke to them and said, "Take heart, it is I; do not be afraid."

Peter answered him, "Lord, if it is you, command me to come to you on the water." He said, "Come." So Peter got out of the boat, started walking on the water, and came toward Jesus.

But when he noticed the strong wind, he became frightened, and beginning to sink, he cried out, "Lord, save me!" Jesus immediately reached out his hand and caught him saying to him, "You of little faith, why did you doubt?" When they got into the boat, the wind ceased. And those in the boat worshiped him, saying, "Truly you are the Son of God."
(Matthew 14:22-32 NRSV)

This Bible story speaks of times of uncertainty, times of not knowing what is ahead. It suggests that the people and the disciples were wondering how to explain the things that happen that both frighten us and make us grieve at the loss of people who are close to us. Just before this particular story is the story of the death of John, called John the Baptist. Jesus was grieving the loss of his close friend John and the disciples were frightened about what it meant for them in the days ahead.

All of us gathered here today know of these times, too, especially as our concern and love for Tracy is shared.

Doug and Lori so clearly embody for me that same kind of willingness to face the unknown that Peter shows in this story. So often in these last few years they have been leading the rest of us in what needed to be faced or discussed or talked about— even though the reality of it all was uncertain and frightening.

But now we stand in another place, and we can look back.

There were many times when the questions were too distressing, the waiting too long, the pain too much—when Doug and Lori could only call out for help—and immediately there was a hand extended, saying, "Take heart. You are not alone."

Sometimes it was the shared grief reflected in each other's eyes, sometimes it was a friend who was willing to come in the middle of the night, sometimes it was a box of food from a stranger, sometimes it was a phone call, and sometimes it was much needed silence.

Was that Jesus reaching out a hand? Oh, yes!

It was Jesus made flesh in many of you—with names like Dawn and Michelle, or Dr. Dave, or Pam and Joel, or Jessie, Jolene and Jill, or Nancy and Sarah and Pat, or Pat and Frank, Collette and Steve, Bob and Laurie, or Troy's friend James—people from work, people from church, and many times it was one of you from this big, loving and caring family.

Sometimes it was Tracy herself who gave the assurance or the comfort to those around her. Tracy was often the courageous, willing person—the leader, the adviser about which direction to take—stepping into her life with eagerness and trust.

You will remember her eyes—so bright and full of light. You will remember her smile—always quick, sometimes shy, but easy to get. You will remember her determination—her insistence on being with the kids for the children's story in church, on the swing in the backyard, or at the table for snacks.

Tracy taught us all about love.

She gave love in trusting so many who were there to help her (though she had a few favorites). She was always smiling and greeting people we might have thought were strangers.

Tracy demanded love.

She needed people around her, and she took strength and spirit from the people who worked with her and who took care of her. She trusted and counted on people in a give-and-take way that made the relationship a healthy one. People always responded to her and gave her what she needed. You are those people.

We were all given the gift of friendship with Tracy because her mom and her dad and her big brother were willing to allow us to receive it. They were willing to share in the giving as well as the receiving. Because of their love and their desire to have the best for Tracy, we have all experienced the unlimited, unending nature of love.

Tracy generated love.

Love grew around her; people responded and still do—not only to her, but also to each other. People who had never met before have shared struggles and grief with each other. Strangers have gotten acquainted, and new friendships have formed.

As we say goodbye to Tracy, we enter into another time of uncertainty for ourselves. Each one of us faces our own fears and pain and grief as we meet the reality of death and the loss of this special child. We might easily fall and be threatened by the waters of doubt and darkness.

Remember the story of Peter and how Jesus immediately reached out his hand to help him and to assure him.

Remember the times you have already passed through.

Remember what you have already endured and how you have been comforted.

Remember how you have been strengthened.

Grieve, but do not be afraid.

The power and love of Jesus, our Risen Savior, is here at hand—very near to you—in our very midst.

We can trust in the goodness and mercy of God all the days of our lives.

Be at peace, Tracy.

And may God's peace be also with all of you. Amen.

Gentle God, you who were born an infant Jesus in the family of Mary and Joseph, we give you thanks for Tracy Ann Ecklund, who was born among us full of hope and promise.

We remember that Jesus lifted children into loving arms to embrace and bless them, and we know that you now hold and bless Tracy as part of your heavenly family.

O God, whose heart aches with our human hurting, we ask for your comfort and your mercy for Tracy's family, for Doug and Lori, her parents, and for Troy, her brother, for her grandparents, aunts, uncles, and cousins. Keep them safe and hopeful in their grieving and in their loneliness. We pray, too, for all the rest of us who mourn today. Grant us your grace and peace in knowing that Tracy is safe and comfortable with you, the Father and Mother of us all. Renew our trust that by your grace our own lives will be brought to fullness in your eternal home.

We ask all this through Jesus Christ, your own beloved child and our risen Savior. Amen.

Summary

Referring to the Crossroads Choices Diagram on page 2, the Crisis Event in this story is the diagnosis of Tracy's brain tumor. The *Chaos* is the response to that diagnosis. Such a diagnosis brings *Chaos* to any family because it introduces so much pain, sorrow and uncertainty. But recently Lori told me of a conversation with her sister nearly eight years after Tracy's death. Her sister wanted to know more about that time, because she had not been able to be there and she had such a dark image in her mind about how it must have been. Lori admitted that there were dark days, but the most vivid memories are of laughter, of Tracy's shy smile, and of how much she loved to see and be with other children.

Lori's image is bright, not dark. And that is because of the choices she and Doug made at the *Crossroads*. They chose to accept the fact that Tracy had been diagnosed with brain cancer even though they had no idea what that would mean to them. They learned along the way about chemo-therapy and brain stem neurological surgery and bone marrow transplants; they learned how to take care of Tracy in their home with IVs and medication, and many hours of simply not knowing what to do. They chose to remain in the uncertainty of each new experience even though it was difficult. They chose to experience it all <u>with</u> Tracy, trusting God to take care of them and doing their best to reassure her in spite of having so many frightening things happening to her. They could have insisted on a clearer picture of what would happen, they could have gotten involved in an academic study of brain cancer and separated themselves from the pain and uncertainty, but they chose to wait and learn what they needed to learn when they needed to know it. They amazed the doctors who worked with them because they were always ready to hear what the doctors had to tell them. It was rarely good news, but they were ready to listen and to respond as they needed to.

Lori and Doug asked me about a funeral director weeks before Tracy died. They wanted to make those arrangements ahead of time. I arranged for a visit in their home, and the funeral director, Steve, helped them make plans for the details of Tracy's death. The day Tracy died, Steve came to their home in a station wagon rather than the usual hearse; he allowed Lori to carry Tracy to the car wrapped in her blanket.

Lori and Doug trusted the process of life and death; they trusted God to help them stay on the very rough road they were traveling. They trusted Tracy to tell them somehow what she needed, and they chose to listen to her. They believe she is the one who taught them about trust.

The nature of such trust is acceptance of uncertainty and confusion. It is the recognition that pain and sorrow and anger and fear and joy—all of them—are part of life. This kind of trust allows others into your life, accepting their help, and lets them share both your pain and your joy. Lori and Doug have discovered that by sharing themselves and their child with others, she continues to be part of life in all those who remember her.

One day, a few months before Tracy died, Lori had taken her to visit her grandparents. Lori had been sitting alone in the living room crying softly when Tracy climbed up beside her and wiggled her way onto her lap.

She took Lori's face in her hands, looked into her eyes, and then gently wiped away her tears. "It will be all right, Momma," she said. And it was, and still is. Very right.

BROKEN BRANCHES

The branches look
white, white against gray
praising creation
grateful for the day
raising limbs to the sky
trying to drink in the sun, the rain, the air.
One branch hangs limply
smaller branches angle off
strangely downward, sideways
at odds with the rest.

Its presence is painful to look at.
Yet, it too is of God:
the product of an unusual break
in a pattern of growth.

A sudden ice storm wreaks havoc
on branches reaching skyward.

Creation is challenged to prune
what is dead
bringing new growth in a new direction
and finding new life
out of what seemed destroyed.

Will God do that with me?

FIVE

CHOICES AND CONSEQUENCES

Will God Do That with Me?

Yes! I believe it! I believe that God, however you describe or understand that entity, lures us, invites us, and urges us to live life fully, to accept "new growth in a new direction."

But God does not do it for us. When we come to the *Crossroads*, we must choose. The way to a full, meaningful life is along a road that includes pain, sorrow, loss, and brokenness. When we follow that road, we will find meaning in life. As we find meaning through the healing we experience, we will also learn to trust God, other people, and to trust the process of life itself. Other choices,

Blaming or *Denying*, draw us away from this particular road and away from God.

I believe that both good and evil are present in the stories I have told. My reflections about these events, particularly the murders, led me to an in-depth study of evil, and Satan in particular. Carl Jung has said, "Evil is terribly real for each and every individual. If you regard the principle of evil as a reality you can just as well call it the devil." While I expand his statement to include calling evil *Satan*, I believe evil is a reality.

Historically, the belief in Satan and evil has been held by the common people, yet denied by church leaders and authorities. Traditionally, the Christian church has believed the importance of proclaiming God as Good as well as Almighty and All-Powerful. But lay people, especially when facing evil or dealing with *Chaos*, have resisted the concept of a good God who was somehow responsible for evil in the world. The concept of Satan or a devil that could be blamed for evil continues to be a popular belief.

As the Christian church became more organized, some groups disagreed with the doctrinal direction the leadership was taking, and the church itself had a need to declare who was right and who was wrong. That was accomplished most directly by suggesting that those who disagreed with the church's official position were aligned with Satan. Since people already understood the concept of Satan as the enemy, Satan became the scapegoat for opposition to orthodox, or accepted, doctrine. Satan was the rallying point used predominantly by the church during the Inquisition, in witch-hunts both in Europe and the United States, and most recently in Satanism.

In this century, political enemies or persons and groups with whom we disagree have been called Satan. This has occurred outside the church and in other countries as well as our own. It has become clear that calling something Satan means that it is evil, potentially dangerous, and is an enemy.

The stories I have related are typical responses to real and very difficult events. They are examples of how ordinary people, some Christian, some not, have reacted to Crisis Events and the *Chaos* that follows. The choices that were made drew some people to different roads away from God. These are the same choices people have made for generations. I believe that such separation from God occurs because of an unexamined understanding of conflicting ideas about God.

If God is All-Powerful, as traditional church doctrine has asserted, then God is responsible for everything, including evil. But, if we believe that God is Good, God could not bring evil. We can avoid this conflicting belief problem by finding something else to blame for the evil we know exists. Perhaps that would be Satan or even what we might label Human Responsibility. However, there is a theological conflict with the designation of another power responsible for evil. Whether or not we acknowledge the conflict, by assigning another power we have declared that God is not All-Powerful. Is that such a difficult concept to accept? If we could be aware of this conflict in our understanding of the power of God, we might be less devastated and more at peace when we sense that God has not answered our prayers or saved our loved ones. It may be that God's powers are limited and we need to re-evaluate our requests and our everyday choices.

Evil is part of our world. We can find many examples of it every day. The difficulty might be our understanding of evil itself. If we believe that evil can somehow be removed once and for all, we will most likely continue to envision God and Satan in a constant battle for the control of human beings. But, if we believe that evil is always with us, then part of our life journey will be to develop the ability to recognize evil in its many forms and to make choices that lead us toward God and away from evil.

I believe it is possible to choose either life or death each moment. It is possible to live through many years, to a "ripe old age," and never to have chosen life. It is also possible to have lived fully every moment of a very short life. Hatred and fear and conflict are evil elements that can grow in human lives and bring about a death in the midst of life. Pointing a finger to others, or even one other, removes personal responsibility for any part of the problem. Choosing to blame moves us away from God and is actually choosing to side with Satan, or choosing death, in the very midst of life.

Satan was the scapegoat. Satan became the reason why such a gruesome thing took place just down the street in Palmyra. At first I thought that if people actually feared the existence of a satanic cult in their town, they would flock to the churches for refuge, and there we would join together to battle evil. But they did not do that. I don't think the people were afraid of Satanism, or even Satan. I think the event itself was so horrible that people could not bear to look at it. They needed something to blame and blaming Satan conveniently took it out of their hands and out of sight.

It didn't matter if the police repeatedly stated they had found nothing to suggest that Satanism was involved in the murders that Chad committed. The general public didn't move to consider any other possibility for Chad's actions. It is entirely possible that a young boy's thwarted sexual overture was the reason for the murders. One newspaper reported that there was evidence of semen in Cindy's body and that the DNA matched Chad Campbell's (Times Union, April 8, 1991). That is a more "earthly" reason for such tragedy, but sex was never mentioned in rumors about the murders.

As a community we might have investigated other possibilities such as the use of drugs or alcohol and, in the process, built a stronger, safer, more trusting community. We might have trusted the uncertainty of not knowing the answers right away, and we might have trusted the power of God in our midst to lead us to find new ways together.

Looking back, I believe we were simply unable to ask questions or take any action together. And I believe it was because those questions or actions would have kept us on the road through the *Chaos*. And that would have kept those murders too real and too unpleasant for too long. That is the stark reality of the difficulty of staying on the road through *Chaos*.

The community was only seeking an answer to the question of why this terrible event had happened. But the resolution of arresting, convicting, and imprisoning the perpetrator brought the answer to the question of who and not why. And that answer did not provide a healing resolution to the town. It may have seemed as if it had, because people stopped talking about it; in fact, after the trial the rumors stopped. Perhaps no one worries any more about any of the issues that were raised by the murders. Except for the families and individuals directly involved, nothing changed for the community. And the people, the elderly, the working, the young, and the children, are no better prepared for the next Crisis Event that breaks into the life of their community. Chances are good that a number of people will say then, as they did before, "I can't believe something like this could happen in this town!"

The desire for an answer and resolution was powerful in my family, too. Perhaps it was a cynical belief that there was no answer that led to the way my parents responded. The absence of a funeral or any kind of tribute to Gary and the reluctance to talk about his death were choices made because of the underlying belief that there was no other way to survive the event of his death.

But there were other ways. We could have had a memorial service of some kind; we could have talked about it and cried together; we could have remembered Gary as a brother and a son who was a significant part of each one of our lives. We could have stayed on the road through the *Chaos* of sorrow and loss, even guilt, and helped one another. We could have grown closer to each other and to God.

We all moved on, covering over the pain. We distanced ourselves from the loss, but our denial was not a healing resolution any more than the people of Palmyra's efforts to place blame. Denial is a choice that leads to death in the very midst of life. It is not choosing life. Evidence of the lack of healing remains in my family. We still find Gary's death difficult to discuss. I believe that in many of the choices I have made as an adult, I have been working through the confusion about life and death that I experienced then.

Tracy's family could easily have chosen blame or denial. They could have blamed any number of things, including Satan or even God, for bringing this illness into their lives and into Tracy's body. They could have spent those few years being angry with an unjust God or the cruel world. They could have denied that Tracy was really so sick and pushed her to try to walk and talk like she could before her surgeries. They could have avoided thinking about her death. They could have denied that it was affecting them, and they could have kept their suffering private. They could have refused to accept anyone's help, not wanting anyone to feel sorry for them. They could have claimed that they were strong enough, and they could have denied their need for support.

But at the *Crossroads,* they chose NOT to blame and NOT to deny. Instead, they chose to *Trust.* And, in the midst of Tracy's struggle and theirs, they had many days of laughter and celebration with Tracy. Their sense of joy and blessing in Tracy's life is even greater than their own experience because they shared their lives, and hers, with so many others. They continue to praise God for all of it!

What made the difference? What made Tracy's family experience so much more life giving than the other two stories I have related? It seems to me that <u>communication</u> and the sense of <u>community</u> are key factors in making a difference. These two elements can provide richness, health, and great joy, but they can also be sources of fear and distrust, as they were both in my family and in the town of Palmyra.

Communication

Silence is a funny thing, especially if we think of it only as the absence of noise. It can be peaceful and restful, but it can also be disturbing. Silence, as the absence of noise and activity, was not a part of my growing up. There was always plenty going on! I like remembering the noise of oatmeal box drums and of my brothers' rowdy games and of story records that we listened to over and over again for hours.

But silence as the absence of communication <u>was</u> part of my growing up; there were definitely some things we just didn't talk about. I don't remember being told not to talk about Gary or about anything else in particular, but I know even now when I've brought up something taboo in my family. My heart races and my hands sweat, and I have difficulty discerning what should be discussed anyway and what should not.

Silence in the church community can also take a repressive form. I learned in my church in Palmyra that no one wanted to discuss the issue of Satan or evil or fears or uncertainties, or even faith in many cases, unless forced to by a personal crisis. As the pastor, that concerned me, because these were all things the church should address. But it was much easier to talk about painting the hallway or keeping the silverware polished, or even paying Conference apportionments (which nobody liked doing <u>or</u> talking about!).

Between the people of Palmyra, there was a peculiar outward silence. Whispered rumors spread like wildfire, and people had plenty to talk about as they speculated about satanic activity around the murder scene, or remembered how many neighborhood cats had disappeared recently, suggesting satanic ritual activity. But, as I have said, there was a silence and an absence of speculation about any other possibility in the murder. Perhaps it can be attributed to an awkward respect for the dead not to discuss possible sexual interest, but the murders were far more damaging than any talk could have been.

Silence, as absence of noise <u>or</u> of communication, was not a feature of Lori and Doug's home. There was shouting and laughter, singing and crying. And all of it was acceptable. Troy was able to listen to his parents and their explanations, but he was able to contradict them and claim his own perspective and needs. He was able to give his truck to Tracy, and that was fine. And he was able to want it back, and that was fine, too. It was all part of the experience of loving and losing Tracy, of life and death, and of that family's life experience. Troy was able to be Troy, not Lori or Doug. He was separate but connected to his parents and to Tracy and, ultimately, to God. He knew he was a child of God.

Community

The concept of community has been part of the Judeo-Christian tradition from the beginning. The laws we still quote, the Ten Commandments, were expressly for the community. Following these laws established a firm base for community living. Breaking them brought trouble to the community because relationships were broken and trust was lost. The power of those laws is based on the individuals' strong desire to be part of the community; they were safer when they were part of a community.

Many people are attracted to church because of a desire to belong to a community. And many leave because the community has disappointed them. It is often because people gossip or fuss or disagree about trivia. But that's what communities do! The way to find resolution to the difficulties that erupt in churches, or in any other community, is the same as that indicated in the Crossroads Choices Diagram. People must stay on the road, *Going Through* the disagreement to work it out; *Getting Over It* by denying it or *Getting Around It* by blaming someone or something leaves issues unresolved. But it is hard to get church communities to be open and honest with one another about their disagreements rather than talking about it privately or in the church parking lot. Most people don't like getting angry or emotional in public. So silence, the unspoken;

exists in communities in the same way it does in some families, and it is a factor of the inability to build a trusting community.

It is true, however, that even though communities and families disappoint and fail, they also have tremendous potential for good. People in churches and in families can often exemplify the very best of why community is so desirable! People gather to celebrate events and share joy in ways that could never be accomplished alone. And there is no substitute for our human ability to support and comfort one another in times of need and sorrow. And sometimes when trust is too difficult and the road is too rough, the community can carry us for a while until we are restored. Furthermore, while shared joy is increased, shared grief can diminish the pain or at the very least, make it bearable.

The communal experience involving Tracy's family and the church community worked because of the openness of the family and the willingness of the church people to be involved with this new family. Because it was such a contrast to my previous experiences, I was in awe of the way both Lori and Doug opened their hearts and lives to people who had been strangers but were part of this church they were now attending. They shared their

74

struggles and joys, and eventually their sadness, with the people of the church. Their openness brought out the best in people. Many people brought food, of course, but they also provided transportation, took care of Troy, sat with Tracy, or just called to say "Hello, we're thinking about you and praying for you."

The sense of community has continued in the years after Tracy died. Lori and Doug have relocated and now their life is full of new activities and a new community. They are involved in a new church community because of the positive experiences they have had in sharing both joy and sorrow with others. This community did not prevent sadness or pain, and I have no doubt that another Crisis Event will be painful for this family. But they have learned powerful lessons about dealing with crisis and *Chaos* and continuing to live. And they have experienced the presence and love of God in their experience of community.

Conclusion

Life has meaning, and the way to find it is to travel through the chaotic mess that follows difficult events and disorients our lives. Those events, and the mess, *are* our lives! The crisis, the feelings, the confusion—*all* of it is what life is about. Feeling, experiencing, living it all means staying on the road of life—our life. Staying on the road is the way to experience trust and to grow in hope. Hope grows in the knowledge that resolution, healing, and new life will come—and because it has come before, it will come again.

Perhaps God is not All-Powerful. God provides comfort and strength and endurance but depends on our responses to address the problems of evil. God is in the midst of community that trusts the unknown, provides support, celebrates life, and is open to new ideas and new solutions to age-old problems. This is what it means to stay on the road through *Chaos*. This is the road of wholeness and life for which we were created. For me, the road itself is God's plan.

When you attempt to stay on the road, you are choosing life, the life God created you to live because you are a *child of God*.

When you face and integrate all of your life experiences, your life becomes one whole, *holy* piece.

FEAR OF THE DARK

It's not the dark that frightens me
but the time before dark
when I imagine
monsters and dangers.

I'm afraid of falling and falling and falling.
I'm afraid of finding no one there.
I'm afraid of getting lost.
I'm afraid of forgetting about light.

But the darkness is never
as scary as my thoughts.

When I can allow soft velvet darkness
to surround me,
release my clutching fingers,
I find blessed holy space.

Quiet.
Gentleness.
YES.

EPILOGUE

FEED THE PEOPLE

A Sermon Delivered August 5, 1990
Palmyra, New York

> *Now when Jesus heard this [the death of John the*
> *Baptist], he withdrew from there in a boat to a deserted*
> *place by himself. But when the crowds heard it, they*
> *followed him on foot from the towns. When he went*
> *ashore, he saw a great crowd; and he had compassion*
> *for them and cured their sick.*
>
> *When it was evening, the disciples came to him and*
> *said, "This is a deserted place, and the hour is now late;*
> *send the crowds away so that they may go into the*
> *villages and buy food for themselves."*
>
> *Jesus said to them, "They need not go away; you give*
> *them something to eat."*

They replied, "We have nothing here but five loaves and two fish." And he said, "Bring them to me." Then he ordered the crowds to sit down on the grass. Taking the five loaves and the two fish, he looked up to heaven, and blessed and broke the loaves, and gave them to the disciples, and the disciples gave them to the crowds. And all ate and were filled; and they took up what was left over of the broken pieces, twelve baskets full. And those who ate were five thousand men, besides women and children.   (Matthew 14:13-20 NRSV)

What Jesus had just learned before he went in the boat off by himself was that his friend, his cousin, his co-worker, John the Baptist had just been killed. He had been beheaded by King Herod's jailers at the whimsical request of a young girl. It was a senseless brutal death. Jesus withdrew because he needed to be alone in prayer with God.

The people of the villages heard the news, too. It must have been frightening to recognize the inhumanity expressed by their political ruler. What could it mean for all of them? They must have been filled with dread, with fear, with grief, with confusion. The people left the villages in great numbers, trying to find Jesus. They desperately wanted to hear what he would say and to see how he was taking it.

And when he saw them, he had compassion on them. Another place in the Bible, Jesus perceives the crowd as sheep without a shepherd, and I imagine the people appeared that way to him in this circumstance as well. And, the scripture says, he cured all their sick.

Jesus understood the need to find answers, the feeling of being lost—he had sought his own refuge with God. He responded out of his own experience that had brought him comfort and grounding. He had compassion for the people who sought his help.

That may have been all they wanted—to be prayed with, to be touched by someone who was so secure in his faith after such a devastating experience that his faith was not shaken loose. But Jesus knew that more was needed.

The disciples also thought that Jesus' healing of the sick was enough. They wanted to protect him, to preserve his energy. They urged him to disperse the crowds so that people could take care of their own needs for food and could be on their way. But Jesus kept them all together and challenged the disciples further when he said, "You feed them."

Anyone would have known that five loaves and two fish were not nearly enough to feed a crowd that size. Anyone would have thought none of the people gathered had enough faith to carry them through the difficult times they faced. But Jesus thought something different. He said by his words and actions to both the disciples and to the crowd gathered there, "You DO have enough! You have enough food, you have enough faith, you have enough among you to live."

He showed them how. He asked for all that was available to be brought to him. And then he thanked God and blessed the food and broke the bread. Then he shared it with the disciples, and directed them to share it with the people.

He trusted God to work right there in their midst. He trusted God that all would be fed.

It could be that the small amount of food was multiplied by God to become food enough for all. Or it could be that closed, fearful hearts were broken open by God, and previously hoarded food was shared among friends and neighbors and strangers who sat together on the grass.

However it was accomplished, everyone ate—every one of them. And they were all satisfied, because there was even some left over.

Jesus did more than respond to those people individually, curing their illnesses. He showed them how to live. He showed them how to trust one another and not to be afraid in spite of the fears they had about the killing.

"You can feed them," he told the disciples.
"You can feed each other," he told the crowd.

Perhaps we can understand the wonder of that miracle more clearly today because of what our own community has been through this past week. We have experienced some of those same feelings of fear and panic and grief and horror. And we, too, have heard the shocking news of death. And we, too, have been forced to see that a human being is capable of inflicting this kind of injury on others.

Perhaps you have wondered where to go for answers. Who can tell us what we need to know? Who can give answers to questions we think are impossible?

Where is God?

How could a loving God allow this to happen?
How can I hang on to my faith in the midst of such
questioning and confusion?

All too often the long-term results of such awful
times are to discard the faith and turn against God
because neither seem to provide answers to this
reality—that death and murder can and do happen.
That response is a tragic loss. For in God is the
very strength that can bring about healing.

It is equally tragic to be captured and overcome by
fear—even though fear is an appropriate response
to danger and is inevitable in light of the
experiences we have faced this week.

But fear can cause us to build barriers between
each other. And fear can make us afraid to trust
anyone—first, strangers, and then even friends,
cannot be trusted. And we gradually begin to
retreat into our houses and lock the doors against
all outsiders.

That may be what we feel like doing in response to
fear. It may even seem to be the most logical
response to this situation. But locking the doors,
separating ourselves from one another, is exactly
what the disciples thought was logical, too. They

wanted everyone to go to their own homes.

But Jesus said, "No!" And I believe Jesus would say the same to us today.

Locking our doors to one another, whether we do it literally or just by locking our hearts, is a response that eventually brings death—death to our community and death to each one of us. It does not protect the life we hoped to protect. How can you live when you are all locked up?

Our only hope for life, and for safety, is to turn to one another, and to God, in trust.

Our only hope for life is to heed the words that are repeated so often, "Do not be afraid!" And the reason they are repeated so often is that those feelings of fear and distrust are very real and very human.

It doesn't mean to ignore the danger or to pretend there is no danger, because we live in dangerous times. We must recognize that our community is not uniquely safe and insulated from the dangers of the rest of the world. And we must take necessary precautions to protect our families as best we can.

85

We can no longer assume that we are all safe here simply because we want things to be that way.

But trusting God and trusting one another means that IF we are willing to face the real problems of our community, then we will have the potential to become what we only hoped we were. We do it by not responding to the fear and by not locking our families and ourselves inside our houses.

We do it by acting in love and in trust, and we work hard to build a safe community by building trust with one another—not just assuming it is already there.

We are seeking LIFE for ourselves, for our families, for our community, and for our world. We all want to experience all that life has to offer. But we are tasting the fear that is death.

Our only hope to survive and to live is to find new ways to become "community."

We must refuse to allow fear to take hold of our hearts. We must encourage the telling of our fears and uncertainties to one another and to get them out in the open where, amazingly enough, they do not seem quite so frightening.

We must no longer deny the isolation that many of our residents have experienced for a long time— both young and old. We must listen to each other's stories and respond with compassion, like Jesus did, to the pain and the grief all around us. We must let the love of God guide us in knowing how to comfort our young people, our grieving neighbors, and our own stirred-up experiences of loss.

We are gathered here together today, together in all our differences, and we are invited to share a meal together. It's a symbolic meal—a meal that reminds us of the source of our strength, of our resources, of our abilities to help each other, and our opportunities to feed each other.

It's a meal that feeds our faith. Whoever would imagine that a scrap of bread and a sip from this cup could ever be enough to satisfy all of us.

But this is a meal filled with the love of God. There is enough for every one of you.

And there will be leftovers to take home.

Praise God!

AWARENESS GUIDE

FOR

THE ROAD THROUGH CHAOS

Introduction

T his guide is designed to increase the awareness of choices that we make every day. Of all the choices we make, none are more essential to our faith, to our outlook, and to our understanding of life itself than the choices we make when our lives are in *Chaos*. When I speak of *Chaos* in this guide, I am particularly interested in the period of time that follows crisis as portrayed in the Crossroads Choices Diagram found in Chapter One.

This guide was developed with the belief that awareness is a basis for change. Awareness of where we are in the process of dealing with Crisis Events and the *Chaos* that follows helps us trust the uncertainty and difficulty of the present moment because we can understand that we are moving through it and we will find healing.

The first part of this book contains three stories of some exceptionally clear ways people have faced *Chaos* and made choices for *Going Through It,*

Getting Around It, or *Getting Over It.* The "holy way" to face this time of *Chaos* is by *Going Through It* on the road that integrates struggle, pain, and trust into life in spite of all the uncertainty that surrounds a difficult time. We choose which road we will follow, but most often that choice is an unconscious one. It is my belief that when we become aware of the choices that are possible and aware of the consequences of those choices, we will be able to make choices for our lives that will lead to health and wholeness.

Choosing to remain on the road is choosing to walk with God. But this choice is the most difficult. So, you might ask, why in the world would we want to choose that road? Because, I believe, that IS the abundant, full, whole life that God has promised!

To the Individual

This is a study of faith. It is also a study of life, *yours.* Your life is the prerequisite for this study. You may work with a group or you may choose to work alone, but the challenge will be to examine your life, your experiences, the choices you have already made at previous *Crossroads,* and then to consider the choices you might have made. The focus is on a positive and hopeful approach to real and difficult times in life. This approach is not designed to make the process of dealing with crisis any easier. But I believe you will be able to see Crisis Events and the resulting *Chaos* from a different perspective that will allow you to be more intentional about the choices you make in the future. It will also make you more hopeful that the difficulty, the *Chaos* in which you find yourself, will pass. The process will strengthen you and life itself will be more meaningful. You will find specific activities for this process in the Awareness Guide.

To the Group Leader

This study of faith may be most beneficial when done with a group because of the support and community that can grow through the process of sharing information and experiences. As group leader, your greatest responsibility is not to be presenter of information, but to be guide and creator of a safe place to discuss difficult experiences. I believe that the material presented in the first part of this book will stimulate memories in each person who reads it and chooses to participate in this study. Your greatest challenge will be to listen with compassion and acceptance. You must know that it is not your job as leader (nor is it possible!) to solve other people's

93

problems or to determine the best course for anyone in the group to follow in their lives. And as leader, you must prevent another group member from trying to do that for anyone else in the group. This is an opportunity for personal growth for each person to determine for him/ herself.

It will also be important for you to state to the group (preferably at the beginning of each session) that it is not a requirement for each person to answer every question or share an experience. Many people learn a great deal by listening to others. However, there are some people for whom conversation and sharing come very easily; these people may tend to dominate and prevent others from speaking. As leader, you must be aware of these group dynamics and gently, but directly, suggest that others may wish to speak.

It is also your responsibility as leader to keep track of time and to move the group to new activities throughout the session. I have suggested that each session be one and one-half hours, but you will determine the specifics depending on the size and interest of your group. You should not let small groups go on too long; it is better that people still have something to say when you call them back to the large group. They are more likely to keep the discussion going in the larger group, which can include everyone. The purpose of the small group is to stimulate discussion that is sometimes difficult to start in a large group. The goal of this kind of group study is the potential community-building that grows as a result of sharing experiences and learning. May you find that experience with your group.

Overview of Awareness Guide

This guide is based on the Principles of Crossroads Choices and the Crossroads Choices Diagram, which are described and explained in Chapter One. This Awareness Guide is presented in six parts following the six principles with specific directions for Group Activities and Activities for the Individual. I have listed a few resources to provide additional information on each principle for more examples or information about the topic under discussion.

Additional resources and more detailed information about the suggested books can be found in the Annotated Bibliography that follows this guide. The Index of Resources by Category will guide you to material of particular interest.

LIFE HAS MEANING

Principle One: Life has meaning and life is chaotic.

Group Activities:

1. Introductions: Each person introduce himself or herself by stating name and a brief statement about what makes life meaningful right now. If time permits after one round, follow with more discussion encouraging members to elaborate on their experience or perspective.

2. Leader Presentation: Post a large copy of the Crossroads Choices Diagram and briefly explain. Chapter One gives information for this presentation.

3. Identifying Crisis Events: Invite group members to reflect quietly and remember various events in their own lives that could be described as "crisis." After a few minutes of quiet, the leader may list these events on newsprint as they are named aloud. After everyone has contributed, allow moments of silence to acknowledge the difficulties experienced in these crises.

4. <u>Individual—then Small Group Discussion</u>:
Invite participants to find space alone for a
personal reflection time of 10-15 minutes on the
questions listed below. Then gather the group
together for reflection on the thoughts
generated. <u>Alternative 1</u>: Use the questions as
"homework" to be discussed at the opening of
the next session. <u>Alternative 2</u>: Use a
combination of activities, discussing one Crisis
Event and a few questions with the group, then
directing members of the group to continue on
their own throughout the week to discuss at the
next session.

Describe a significant Crisis Event in your life.

- How did you or did you not experience
  God in that event?

- Did that experience influence your
  understanding of God? How?

- What is your understanding of God at
  this time in your life?

- What would you like to ask of God? What
  do you pray for?

5. <u>Closing</u>: Gather as a group and invite anyone to
speak in closing; could be a summary of what

has been said, or a blessing of life experiences, or prayers for what is still needed for those who have suffered.

Activities for the Individual:
You will need a notebook to use as a journal for this process of awareness. Before you begin, review the Crossroads Choices Diagram (page 2) and the Principles of Crossroads Choices (page 10). Personal Reflection: Thinking back over the course of your life, make a list of the Crisis Events that have been part of your experience. Select one Event that was significant and write out your answers to the questions listed under Group Activities #4. End your writing session with a written prayer stating what you most need at this time.

Additional Resources:

The Wisdom of Insecurity, Alan W. Watts

Storytelling: Imagination and Faith, William J. Bausch

St. George and the Dragon, and the Quest for the Holy Grail, Fr. Edward Hays

DEFINING CHAOS

Principle Two: We can choose how to face Chaos.

Group Activities: (Start each session with the opportunity to discuss whatever was generated in thoughts throughout the past week as a result of the previous session.)

1. Group definition of *Chaos:*

♦ Write on newsprint—from the group generate words, ideas, and concepts of *Chaos.*

Consider specific events or activities as well as words that define *Chaos.*
Include biblical understandings: i.e., turbulent or stormy waters, evil.
Dictionary definitions: "1) Any condition or place of total disorder or confusion. 2) *Often capital C.* The disordered state of unformed matter and infinite space supposed by some religious cosmological views to have existed prior to the ordered universe." (American Heritage Dictionary of the English Language. Houghton-Mifflin Company. 1969)

2. Small Group Discussion: Divide into groups of 2 or 3 to discuss the sentence, "Life is chaotic."

♦ Questions to consider either as small groups or as personal reflection and then to share with large group (allow 2-3 minutes for reflection).

General: What in your life is chaotic, or what makes it chaotic?
Specific: Describe the *Chaos* you experienced after a Crisis Event. How did you feel? What was going on in your mind, in your family, at work? You may want to share how you reacted and what you did.

3. Large Group Discussion: Report to large group on experiences or thoughts shared in small groups.

4. Closing: Gather as a large group and invite someone to summarize or comment based on the discussions, or allow individuals to speak to close as they wish.

Activities for the Individual
In your notebook journal write out your experience of *Chaos* in descriptive detail; then examine what you have written and consider your experience based on the questions from Group Activity #2.

Additional Resources:

<u>Psalm 139:1-3</u> is a biblical expression of *Chaos*. Read together and talk about the *Chaos* described or use as personal reflection. Does this capture your experience?

<u>The Gift of Fear</u>, Gavin de Becker: Fear is often a component of *Chaos*. The author discusses the nature of fear and how it can help us identify potential crises in order to prevent them.

<u>Den of Lions</u>, Terry Anderson: Terry Anderson was taken as hostage in Lebanon and held captive, often in chains and blindfolded, for seven years. This is his reflection on that experience. The book includes poems written while he was a captive and might be helpful to use to start a discussion. A powerful description of *Chaos* and his story is full of hope as he describes how he survived.

BLAMING

Principle Three: Getting Around It means blaming someone or something for the event that has disrupted your life.

Group Activities:

1. <u>Getting Started</u>: With the group gathered together, after initial greetings are given, make a brief presentation of the topic *BLAMING*.

Suggestion: *From the very first story of human beings in the Bible, the story of Adam and Eve, it seems that we humans find it necessary at times to blame someone or something outside of ourselves.On the surface, eating an apple may not seem like a crisis, but Adam felt sufficiently threatened by God's questions to point a finger to Eve who pointed to the serpent! While you may question the literal truth of this biblical story, you must certainly agree that it expresses a truth about human beings!*

It seems that there are situations or circumstances that are so difficult or so terrible (or somehow so threatening) that we feel we must try to explain them—or try to name who or what it is that caused this awful event. Perhaps we simply need to find a

focus for the anger and frustration we feel as we
face a situation we cannot control.

Still in the large group, begin to generate from the
group the various persons or entities that might be
the focus of blame. Ask for the circumstances and
the words that might be said to show blame.

Examples: *a spouse, a best friend, a known enemy*
(personal animosity), or an unknown one (like
people or groups you have never met), God, Satan,
self, parent or parents, HMO or doctor or hospital,
another race or ethnic group, etc.

2. <u>Individual—then Small Group Discussion</u>:
   Take 10-15 minutes for personal reflection.
   Thinking back on crisis experiences in your life,
   try to identify someone or something you might
   have blamed (even if only temporarily) for the
   event; for instance, you might have blamed
   yourself or some other person, or the
   circumstance, etc. Using the Crossroads Choices
   Diagram and following the arrow off the road in
   attempting to blame someone or something,
   think about where that led you. Did it make
   you angry? Did it bring you consolation? Did it
   assist you in your dealing with the event? Why
   or why not? Did it lead you to any decisions or

answers about your life or your family or your faith? What happened if you blamed yourself— did it ease the pain or did it bring you closer to others?

Now gather in groups of 2 or 3 to share your experiences and insights of blame. Each group might consider how blaming helped (or did not help) in dealing with the Crisis Event. Consider whether or not it brought about healing or health in the community involved in the crisis— whether that is a couple or a family or a whole town. Why or why not was healing achieved?

3. Large Group Discussion: We often describe those we blame as *enemy*. Generate a list of potential enemies of members of the group— they can have specific names, or just be categories (like "my neighbor"). Identify what it is that you blame your enemy for—try to be specific. Extended Discussion: What does "Love your enemies" mean to you in this context? What do you think Jesus meant by that statement? If there is time, consider various understandings of *Forgiveness*. Is it possible? Is it required of us as followers of Jesus? Or of us as human beings? How is it achieved?

4. <u>Closing</u>: Follow whatever pattern has been established.

Activities for the Individual

Review the section on the topic BLAMING in Group Activities #1. Write your own list of persons or entities that might be the focus of blame along with the words or circumstances that might bring about a desire to place blame. Then, reflecting on your past Crisis Events, try to identify someone or something you might have blamed (even if only temporarily) for the event. Write out your thoughts using the questions in #2 as suggestions.

Think about the idea of *enemy*. We often consider someone we blame an enemy. Write out an experience where you might have felt that someone you blamed was an enemy. Think about Jesus' statement, "Love your enemies." What do you think he meant? How would it apply to your circumstance?

Think about your understanding of *forgiveness*. Relate it in your writing to what you have said about *blame* and *enemy*. Is forgiveness always required of us as followers of Jesus? Is it possible? How can we achieve it?

105

Additional Resources:

<u>The Old Enemy: Satan and the Combat Myth</u>, Neil Forsyth. One ancient understanding of Satan is that of *enemy* who can be blamed for evil in the world. This book is an academic study which includes a look at literature, biblical and extra-biblical material and presents an array of information about Satan and *enemy*.

<u>Dark Nature</u>, Lyall Watson. This is a book about biology and human development, but the author is seeking an answer to the question of evil. He examines a number of situations (both animal and human) and discusses the source and presence of evil in life.

The story of the Prodigal Son, Luke 15:11-32

DENYING

Principle Four: Getting Over It is denying that this event is part of your life or that it is important in your life.

Group Activities:

1. <u>Getting Started</u>: Following greetings, the leader should make an introduction of the topic *DENYING*.

   Suggestion: *Denial might be as clear as saying, "I didn't do it." Or it might be as elusive as erasing something from a page, or declaring that something that has happened to you is really not that important—when that same experience would be devastating to another in similar circumstances.*

   The "denial" we are talking about here is a result of several things. One is the expectation that life should be good and perfect, and if anything bad or imperfect happens, it is not part of real life. The person that holds this kind of expectation of life will most certainly feel that the appropriate response is to get over "it" as quickly as possible.

Part of this response is the attempt to control things, events, feelings, and actions.

The second thing that might bring about denial in response to crisis is fear—fear of feeling the strong, disorienting, and painful feelings of hurt, loss, loneliness, and uncertainty. It is possible to protect yourself from these feelings, but the cost is distance from other people, even those who are important to you.

2. <u>Large Group Discussion—then Small Group</u>: Read aloud the list of statements below that can be examples of denial; add any others the group can generate. Divide list and then divide into groups of 3-4 to discuss the questions that follow the statements.

- I don't know him. (What Peter said about Jesus.)
- I'm fine.
- Oh, it's not that important.
- It's not that big a deal.
- It's water over the dam.
- Let's not talk about it.
- Let's move on.
- I'm tired of talking about it.
- It's God's will that this happened.

- I just need to get on with my life.
- He/she didn't really mean it (the harsh words, angry act, drunken fight, etc.)
- He/she is sick.

How are these acts or words of denial? What do they deny? How do they separate the person saying them from the event or from potential healing? What is the person really saying— under the words? Where do they lead the speaker—toward something or away from something?

3. Personal Reflection: Consider times when you might have been in denial. What words did you use? How did those words protect you? How did denial help or hurt you in dealing with the crisis event? Was fear a factor? Fear of what? What was uncertain or unknown in your experience?

4. Group Listening: Invite individuals to discuss their experience and their perception of how denial affected them.

5. Closing: Brief sharing as a closing or remain in simple silence together before departing.

Activities for the Individual:

Read over the material on DENIAL in Group Activities #1. List the statements in #2 in your notebook journal and answer the questions that follow the statements.

Do Activity #3, Personal Reflection writing in your notebook journal; reflect on how denial affected you.

Additional Resources:

All of these resources deal specifically with the topic of *denial*.

People of the Lie, F. Scott Peck

Dance of Deception, Harriet G. Lerner

Addiction and Grace, Gerald G. May

The Gift of Fear, by Gavin de Becker

TRUSTING

Principle Five: Going Through It is going through the middle of the chaos on the road of your life, trusting that you will find healing in the process.

Group Activities:

1. Getting Started: Read aloud the story of the Prodigal Son in Luke 15:11-32. This story is often discussed as an example of God, but in this situation, ask listeners to find examples of trust between human beings—two very different sons and a father. List them on newsprint or board as they are identified. Why do you think they are examples of trust—what else could have happened in each instance?

2. Small Group Activity: Divide into small groups, giving each group one word (see below) to define and come up with an example to share with the whole group. The example can be a real one from someone's experience, a biblical example, or a created one. Questions for each word are included simply to help get a discussion started; it is not necessary to answer every question if the group is talking.

Trust: Define *Trust*, then consider: What does it mean to trust another person? What do you expect when you trust someone? What is real about trust and what might be naïve? What does it mean to trust God? What does it mean to "trust the process"?

Hope: Define *Hope*, then consider: Is "hope" the same as "wish" or is hope based on something deeper? What would that be? What does this Bible verse mean to you?

Romans 8:24-25: Now hope that is seen is not hope. For who hopes for what is seen? But if we hope for what we do not see, we wait for it with patience.

Do you hope FOR something or do you HAVE hope? What's the difference?

Grace: Define *Grace*, then consider: How do we experience grace? Does everyone experience grace or just special people? Can it be explained? How do we get it? Where does it come from?

Healing: Define *Healing*, then consider: Name different kinds of healing. Is there more than one possible healing in sickness or broken relationships or brokenness? Who determines

healing? If I say, I AM HEALED, is it true?
Can we observe healing? What does it look like?

Child of God: Discuss your understanding of this
concept. Is it something you consider in your
relationship to God? What does it mean in your
relationship to other people? Is everyone a
"child of God"?

3. Large Group Discussion: After the sharing of
   information regarding words, if the groups have
   not already moved to personal sharing,
   determine whether to move to large group or to
   stay in smaller groups to talk about personal
   experiences of each of these areas: trust, hope,
   grace, healing.

4. Closing: Let the group determine closing
   procedure before departing.

Activities for the Individual:
Read aloud the story of the Prodigal Son in your
Bible, Luke 15: 11-32. Watch for examples of trust
between the characters—two very different sons
and a father. Write them in your notebook journal.

Write out your reflections on each of the topics listed in Group Activity #2. Let the questions quide your thoughts.

Additional Resources:

Although these resources are not specifically about trust, each author discusses relationships between people and with God. The poetry and the reflections of these authors will surely enrich your own reflection.

Dakota: A Spiritual Geography, Kathleen Norris

Coming to Life: Traveling the Spiritual Path of Everyday Life, Polly Berrien Berends

Den of Lions, Terry Anderson

COMMUNITY AND CONNECTION
MAKING THE CHOICE

Principle Six: The way to find meaning in life is to go through the Chaos.

Group Activities:

1. Getting started: Have the Crossroads Choices Diagram on display; review the choices and where they lead: *Getting Over It* or Blaming leads to Isolation; *Getting Around It* or Denying leads to Isolation; *Going Through It* or Trusting leads to healing and connection with self, with others, and with God.

2. Personal Reflection: Before group discussion, allow time alone. Ask group members to think back over the Crisis Events that have been remembered (particularly one's own experiences) during the course of these discussions. Focus on one that was especially difficult. Realizing it is possible to try all three of the paths discussed here, try to remember if you made any or all of the choices in response to the *Chaos* following the Crisis Event. What were the choices possible in that experience to

115

show blame, denial, or trust? (Maybe you actually made them, maybe you didn't.) What new insights do you have about the choices made or not made?

As a result of your experience and your response, consider aspects of good and evil. Was either represented in any way in your experience? How do you think God was part of your experience? Was God involved at all? How would you describe God at this point in your life?

Consider the aspects of <u>communication</u> and <u>community</u> that you did or did not experience as a result of your choice. What did you do that opened or closed communication with others around you? What were your experiences of isolation and experiences of community? Do you wish it had turned out differently than it did? What healing did you hope for? What might you have done to make a difference?

3. <u>Large Group Sharing</u>: Gather together to share as desired about individual reflections and insights into your experiences and understanding. Are there ways community and

communication have been helped or made possible through this study and reflection?

4. Closing: Read Deuteronomy 30:19 and Isaiah 43:1b-3a, 4a. Invite closing prayers as desired by the group. (The group might wish to consider whether additional sessions are desirable.)

Activities for the Individual:
Look at the Crossroads Choices Diagram on page 2 and re-read the Principles listed on page 10. Follow the questions and suggestions in Group Activity #2 as you think back over the Crisis Events you have remembered in your notebook journal. Continue to write reflecting on the questions about good and evil, communication and community.
Read Deuteronomy 30:19 and Isaiah 43:1b-3a, 4a. Return to these verses often as reminders that God is with you and always loves you.

Additional Resources:

The Psalms, Kathleen Norris

A Biblical Example: Chapter One, Crossroads Choices: Confronting Chaos (page 11)

Epilogue: "Feed the People" Crossroads Choices: Confronting Chaos (page 79)

INDEX

RESOURCES
BY
CATEGORY

(Note: This list enables the reader to find author and title by subject or category and then locate more information in the Annotated Bibliography section. Some books are listed in more than one category.)

Autobiography
Anderson, Terry **Den of Lions: A Startling Memoir of Survival and Triumph**

Bible Study Resources
Bright, John **The Authority of the Old Testament**

Cobb, John/et al **Biblical Preaching on the Death of Jesus**

Eichrodt, Walther **Theology of the Old Testament** (2 volumes)

Griggs, Donald L. **20 New Ways of Teaching the Bible**

Griggs, Patricia **Using Storytelling in Christian Education**

Hanson, Paul D. **The People Called: The Growth of Community in the Bible**

Klassen, William **Love of Enemies: The Way to Peace**

Kushner, Harold **When Bad Things Happen to Good People**

Murray, Dick **Teaching the Bible to Adults and Youth**

Nolan, Albert **Jesus Before Christianity**

Perkins, Pheme **Reading the New Testament**

Perrin, Norman/ Duling, Dennis **The New Testament: An Introduction—Proclamation and Parenesis, Myth and History**
Stendahl, Krister **Paul Among the Jews and Gentiles**
Terrien, Samuel **The Elusive Presence**
Westermann, Claus **Elements of Old Testament Theology**
Wink, Walter **Transforming Bible Study**

Encyclopedias and Bibles
Cavendish, Richard **Man, Myth and Magic: The Illustrated Encyclopedia of Mythology, Religion and the Unknown**
Jackson, Guida M. **Encyclopedia of Traditional Epics**

Evil and Satan
Davis, Stephen T. (editor) **Encountering Evil: Live Options in Theodicy**
Delbanco, Andrew **The Death of Satan: How Americans Have Lost the Sense of Evil**
Forsyth, Neil **The Old Enemy: Satan and the Combat Myth**
Pagels, Elaine **The Origin of Satan** and **Adam, Eve and the Serpent**
Passantino, Bob and Gretchen **Satanism**
Peters, Ted **"Satanism: Bunk or Blasphemy"**

Poling, James **The Abuse of Power: A Theological Problem**

Russell, Jeffery Burton **The Devil: Perceptions of Evil from Antiquity to Primitive Christianity**

Sakheim, David K. and S. Devine **Out of Darkness: Exploring Satanism and Ritual Abuse**

Stanford, Peter **The Devil: A Biography**

Watson, Lyall **Dark Nature: A Natural History of Evil**

History/Sociology

Bratton, Fred Gladstone **Myths and Legends of The Ancient Near East**

Cross, Whitney **The Burned-Over District: Social And Intellectual History of Enthusiastic Religion in Western New York, 1800-1850**

Eaton, Harold **"Thanksgiving Sermon"**

Melton, J. Gordon, Ed. **Encyclopedia Handbook of Cults in America**

Michalowski, Kazimierz **Palmyra**

Pagels, Elaine **The Gnostic Gospels**

Perrin, Norman/Duling, Dennis **The New Testament: An Introduction Proclamation and Parenesis, Myth and History**

Poling, James **The Abuse of Power: A Theological Problem**

Robinson, James M. (editor) **The Nag Hammadi Library**

Stendahl, Krister **Paul Among the Jews and Gentiles**
Troskosky, Betty (editor) **Palmyra: A Bicentennial Celebration: 1789-1989**
VanderWall, Col. Edward **New York State Police Report, August 1, 1990 (Chad Campbell Murder Investigation)**
Watson, Lyall **Dark Nature: A Natural History Of Evil**
Westermann, Claus **Elements of Old Testament Theology**

Literature
Koontz, Dean **Midnight** (and other stories)
Norris, Kathleen **Dakota: A Spiritual Geography**

Preaching Resources
Cobb, John (et al) **Biblical Preaching on the Death of Jesus**
McClendon, James **Making Gospel Sense to a Troubled Church**
Nolan, Albert **Jesus Before Christianity**
Stendahl, Krister **Paul Among the Jews and Gentiles**

Spiritual Growth
Berends, Polly Berrien **Coming to Life: Traveling The Spiritual Path in Everyday Life**

Fowler, James **Stages of Faith: The Psychology of Human Development and the Quest for Meaning**
Kushner, Harold **When Bad Things Happen to Good People**
McCullough, Donald **The Trivialization of God: A Dangerous Illusion of a Manageable Diety**
Nolan, Albert **Jesus Before Christianity**
Norris, Kathleen **Dakota: A Spiritual Geography** and **The Cloister Walk**
Phillips, J.B.   **Your God Is Too Small**
Rupp, Joyce   **Fresh Bread**
Westberg, Granger   **Good Grief**
Watts, Alan W.   **The Wisdom of Insecurity: A Message for an Age of Anxiety**

Storytelling

Bausch, William J.   **Storytelling, Imagination and Faith**
Boomershine, Thomas   **Story Journey: An Invitation to the Gospel as Storytelling**
Griggs, Patricia   **Using Storytelling in Christian Education**
Hays, Edward   **St. George and the Dragon and the Quest for the Holy Grail**
Wangerin, Walter, Jr.   **Ragman and Other Cries of Faith**
Wink, Walter **Transforming Bible Study**

Theological/Psychological

Augsburger, David **Helping People Forgive**

Berry, Carmen Renee **When Helping You Is Hurting Me: Escaping the Messiah Trap**

Borysenko, Joan **Guilt Is the Teacher, Love Is the Lesson**

Bridges, William **Transitions**

DeBecker, Gavin **The Gift of Fear: Survival Skills That Protect Us from Violence**

Fox, Matthew **Original Blessing**

Kushner, Harold **When Bad Things Happen to Good People**

Lerner, Harriet G. **The Dance of Anger: A Woman's Guide to Changing the Patterns of Intimate Relationships** and **The Dance of Deception: Pretending and Truth-telling in Women's Lives**

Lester, Andrew **Hope in Pastoral Care and Counseling**

McClendon, James Wm., Jr. **Making Gospel Sense to a Troubled Church**

McCullough, Donald **The Trivialization of God: The Dangerous Illusion of a Manageable Diety**

May, Gerald **Addictions and Grace**

Nolan, Albert **Jesus Before Christianity**

Norris, Kathleeen **Dakota: A Spiritual Geography**

Poling, James **Abuse of Power: A Theological Problem**

Phillips, J.B. **Your God Is Too Small**

Watts, Alan   **The Wisdom of Insecurity: A Message for an Age of Anxiety**

Westberg, Granger E.   **Good Grief**

ANNOTATED
BIBLIOGRAPHY

ANDERSON, Terry. 1993. *Den of Lions: A Startling Memoir of Survival and Triumph.* New York: Ballantine Books. A moving recollection of the seven years Terry Anderson spent in captivity in the Middle East. A journalist for the Associated Press, he was taken prisoner in March 1985 and was assured that it was "only political." This book is a collection of the memories of those horrors, challenges to his humanity and his faith, which he summarizes in poetry that captures the hopelessness, fear, and frustration. Underlying it all is a depth of faith and hope that is astonishing and inspiring for anyone dealing with chaos.

AUGSBURGER, David W. 1996. *Helping People Forgive.* Louisville, Kentucky: Westminster John Knox Press. The author claims that this is his third book on forgiveness and that he will probably write more. Forgiveness is difficult and complex, he says, and his examination includes biblical and psychological and theological analyses. This is a study of blame, denial and reconciliation directed at people who counsel others, but it would be beneficial to a lay person wanting more depth and analysis of the complexity involved in relationships, brokenness and getting to reconciliation.

BAUSCH, William J. 1984. *Storytelling: Imagination and Faith.* Mystic, Connecticut: Twenty-Third Publications.

Publications. A delightful, powerful collection of stories from both Jewish and Christian storytelling traditions, this book also includes a discussion of how stories inform our faith and our understanding of God.

BEARDSLEE, William; COBB, John B.; LULL, David J. 1990. *Biblical Preaching on the Death of Jesus.* Nashville: Abingdon Press. A group of theologians contribute analyses of the gospels starting with the death of Jesus. A very helpful study for the preacher trying to connect theology to real life situations for those in the pews.

BERENDS, Polly Berrien. 1990. *Coming to Life: Traveling the Spiritual Path in Everyday Life.* San Francisco: Harper & Row Publishers. Teaching readers about how to be aware and open to every moment, the author claims "everything that happens is either a blessing that is also a lesson, or a lesson that is also a blessing." She calls these "blessons" and invites us to see all of life for what it is and what we are to discover.

BERRY, Carmen Renee. 1988. *When Helping You is Hurting Me: Escaping the Messiah Trap.* San Francisco: Harper & Row Publishers. A subtle trap for even the most careful pastors, this is relevant to anyone who wants to help other people whether a friend or a client. This is an invitation to the helper to "heal thyself."

BOOMERSHINE, Thomas E. 1988. *Story Journey: An Invitation to the Gospel as Storytelling.* Nashville: Abingdon Press. The author states that "...at the deepest and most profound level, the stories of our lives are empowered and given meaning by being connected with God's story." It is possible to do that when we know God's story so well that we can tell it from memory This book is a "how-to" guide to that kind of memorization with follow-up study of each biblical story and how we might make the connection to our own life story. This is a good guide for a Bible study group or for an individual wanting to be more involved in the stories of the Bible.

BORYSENKO, Joan. 1990. *Guilt is the Teacher, Love is the Lesson.* New York: Warner Books, Inc. Contrasting healthy guilt and shame (which disables), the author examines the lessons that can be learned from the struggles of the spirit. Her work is both psychological and theological as she emphasizes the importance of the spiritual aspects of our lives. She touches on the desolation of what she calls "spiritual pessimism" defined as absolute hopelessness experienced when people believe they are so bad that God is punishing them. She provides a chapter of spiritual exercises and resources at the end of the book.

BRATTON, Fred Gladstone. 1970. *Myths and Legends of the Ancient Near East.* New York: Thomas Y.

Crowell Co. Professor Bratton has taught Biblical languages and literature at Boston University School of Theology, History of Religions at the University of Rochester, and Biblical Literature and Near Eastern Archeology at Springfield College in Massachusetts. The book contains "great stories of the Sumero-Akkadian, Egyptian, Ugaritic, Canaanite and Hittite cultures." It is a good collection of these ancient myths that have influenced western thought and religious ideas. The author is an enthusiastic teacher and his writing is easily read and understood by the lay person.

BRIDGES, William. 1980. *Transitions*. Reading, Massachusetts, Addison-Wesley Publishing Co. A popular book that examines life's changes, from endings, through the transition to new beginnings. Bridges gives strategies and helpful case stories to assist in the process of change.

BRIGHT, John. 1967. *The Authority of the Old Testament*. Grand Rapids, Michigan: Baker Book House. Christians claim that their ultimate authority is God, but what would we know of God if it were not for the Bible? And what would we know of God if it were not for the Old Testament, the basis of the New Testament? In this academic study of the Old Testament, the author builds a case for preaching and worship to be based on the Old Testament. He strongly states that preaching should be biblical and claim the authority of the Word of God.

CARLSON, Richard and BAILEY, Joseph. 1998. *Slowing Down to the Speed of Life: How to Create a More Peaceful, Simpler Life from the Inside Out.* New York: HarperCollins Publishers, Inc. This book applies easily to the principles and diagram presented in my book. The details and simple guidelines for "free-flow thinking" will keep you on the road through the chaos if you trust the process of that experience. If you can't seem to trust, do the suggestions anyway and trust will come! It is when we apply "analytical thinking to problems for which we do not have all the information" that we fall into the patterns of blaming and denial. This book helped me put more specifics to my own ideas and I am most grateful to the authors!

CAVENDISH, Richard. 1995 (First Edition 1970) *Man, Myth and Magic: The Illustrated Encyclopedia of Mythology, Religion and the Unknown.* New York: Marshall Cavendish Corporation Publisher. This twenty-one volume set includes a one-volume index that cross-references the material; a study index lists material by subjects that relate directly to major themes on these topics. The encyclopedia presents pictures, diagrams and historical information on these broad topics.

CROSS, Whitney R. 1950. *The Burned Over District: Social and Intellectual History of Enthusiastic*

Religion in Western New York, 1800-1850. Ithaca, New York: Cornell University Press. Though this is a doctoral thesis, specific to the particular area in which the stories of this book take place, it is a fascinating study of the sociological impact of religion on the development of our culture nationwide.

DAVIS, Stephen T., ed. COBB, John B. Jr., GRIFFIN, David R., HICK, John H., ROTH, John K., SONTAG, Frederick. 1981. *Encountering Evil: Live Options in Theodicy.* Atlanta: John Knox Press. An especially helpful book for a new pastor trying to explain evil to parishioners asking Why? or Why me? This book is a collection of traditional opinions about the problem of evil presented by philosophers and theologians who teach at the Claremont Colleges in Claremont, California. Each contributor presents his own belief about God and the presence of evil in the world from the Judeo-Christian perspective; a section of critiques of that position is presented by fellow colleagues and the final section of each segment gives the original author a chance to respond to the criticism. The postscript discusses the problem of evil and the problems a pastor might encounter as a result of the reality of evil when it seems so present in real lives. The footnotes give further explanation and resources, and the bibliography at the end of the book lists other materials written by each of the writers on the subject of evil.

DE BECKER, Gavin. 1997. *The Gift of Fear: Survival Skills that Protect Us From Violence.* New York: Little, Brown and Company. In a book that is very relevant for this age of violence, Gavin de Becker discusses how we already know much of what would protect us—we need to acknowledge it and act on it. We often hear that no one ever suspected that a particular person was capable of such violence; but it is possible to predict—and prevent—if we learn which behaviors are clues. In this gripping book filled with actual accounts, Mr. De Becker outlines what to look for, how to behave and how to protect yourself. His organization works with highly visible people from entertainment and government. His best gift is empowerment as he looks at the reality of violence and at the awareness of fear that should be heeded. This is a bold criticism of the denial that prevents people from protecting themselves. When we become aware of feelings and can trust intuition, we are free to live and free from excessive and frantic fear that prevents us from seeing and experiencing the good aspects of life, which are abundant in our world.

DELBANCO, Andrew. 1995. *The Death of Satan: How Americans Have Lost the Sense of Evil.* New York: Farrar, Straus and Giroux. Our ancestors envisioned the world as a cosmic battle between good and evil, but the world has changed and scholars, philosophers and theologians have had varied approaches to the problem of evil. Delbanco gives an in-depth study of these views and claims that now we are caught between the ancient and modern views with no clear understanding of how to explain the presence of evil in our midst. That confusion has left us unable to cope effectively with the problems we face. His book is a call to discover new clarity and understanding.

EATON, Harold. 1857. *Thanksgiving Sermon*. Delivered November 26, 1857 at First Presbyterian Church, Palmyra, New York. Published at the request of the Descendants of the First Settlers of Palmyra. On microfiche at the Library of Iliff School of Theology in Denver, Colorado. This sermon is a depiction of the beginnings of the town of Palmyra, NY—from land divided as part of the settlement between the US government and Indian tribes who had originally occupied the land to a significant town along the new Erie canal.

FOWLER, James W. 1981. *Stages of Faith: The Psychology of Human Development and the Quest for Meaning*. San Francisco: HarperSan Francisco (A Division of Harper Collins Publishers). An examination of faith as a dynamic and changing aspect of human life. Fowler presents a theory of seven stages of faith, explaining that, while this theory may clarify our understanding, it might also limit our ability to see beyond what is described. This is a good study book for a church helping people

understand where their current faith fits into a
continuum and encouraging them to grow to new
understandings. Fowler encourages questions and
doubts as part of the process of coming to a new and
relevant faith.

FOX, Matthew. 1983. *Original Blessing: A Primer in
Creation Spirituality*. Santa Fe, New Mexico: Bear
and Company. Giving contemporary examples and
new explanations, Fox explains a very ancient
understanding of God, Creation, good and evil, sin
and blessing. The appendix shows a comparison of
many of these concepts to the church's traditional
understanding of "fall-redemption", or Original Sin—
the reason for the title. Fox has written many other
books since this book was published and has been
"silenced" by the Catholic Church repeatedly for his
unorthodox theology.

GRIGGS, Donald L. 1979. *20 New Ways of Teaching the
Bible*. Nashville: Abingdon Press. A collection of
creative ways to approach the Bible in group or
individual study. Each lesson includes an
introduction, preparation for the leader if needed, and
an outline of steps that could be used to compare
conflicting stories in the Bible, get acquainted with
many of the biblical people, look at prayers or
portrayals of special people of the Bible, or examine
particular themes. There are often worksheets or
questionnaires that can be used with a group. Some

chapters give a variety of approaches that might be used to introduce material to a group. A helpful list of resources and how to get them is included at the back of the booklet.

GRIGGS, Patricia. 1981. *Using Storytelling in Christian Education*. Nashville: Abingdon Press. This is a helpful guide to using stories to teach—it gives suggestions for a teacher to learn how to tell stories and how to use stories in class, but also suggests that learning to tell and use stories might be helpful for students as well. Full of exercises, activities and games, and resources for good stories beyond the Bible organized by categories.

HANSON, Paul D. 1987. *The People Called: The Growth of Community in the Bible*. San Francisco: Harper & Row, Publishers. This is a discussion of the concept of "community" as portrayed throughout the entire Bible. Scholar and writer Phyllis Trible of Union Theological Seminary says, "This scholarly work discloses a faith that is very much in the world through not of it." An excellent resource for preaching research or Bible study or for a deeper understanding of the concept of "community."

HAYS, Edward. 1986. *St. George and the Dragon and the Quest for the Holy Grail*. Easton, Kansas: Forest of Peace Books, Inc. This collection of stories is not included in the list of resources used by Griggs above, but it should be. Placed in a fictitious story of one man's quest for meaning, a dragon tells stories that guide him to understanding.

JACKSON, Guida M., ed. 1994. *Encyclopedia of Traditional Epics*. Santa Barbara, California: ABC-CLIO, Inc. This guide gives background information on many ancient myths and epics with historical information regarding their discovery. The stories are presented in English.

KLASSEN, William. 1984. *Love of Enemies: The Way to Peace*. Philadelphia: Fortress Press. Although Klassen does not work with every text that discusses his topic of peace in the Bible, he does work with significant passages from both the Old and New Testaments. This is an academic exegesis of the topics of peace and love of enemy with solid background information and interpretation of the passages.

KOONTZ, Dean. 1989. *Midnight*. New York: G.P. Putnam's Sons. This is only one of the books I have read by Koontz. He often deals with the conflict of good and evil and includes a theological statement of his understanding somewhere in the story. His books are often dark and gloomy pictures of a world that seems impossible to change or from which to escape—but hope is always discovered in a positive portrayal of the power of resurrection! In all the stories by Koontz that I have read, I have found characters who portray the goodness of creation and who trust that they will find the answers to solve the problems they face—even when they cannot see the answers from the beginning. They are all examples of staying on the road through the chaos in order to find healing and new life!

KUSHNER, Harold. 1983. *When Bad Things Happen to Good People.* New York: Avon Books. This is a tiny book powerfully written....and one I have given to many people, both friends and parishioners. Rabbi Kushner includes an analysis of the Book of Job — often a confusing story for people who can so easily identify with Job and his sense of justice and injustice. He also addresses the problem confronting logical human beings of the conflict of a good God who allows evil or bad things. He speaks from a very personal experience acknowledging his own questions about God's justice. This is a realistic and very helpful study of questions we all have when "bad things" happen in our lives.

LERNER, Harriet G. 1985. *The Dance of Anger: A Woman's Guide to Changing the Patterns of Intimate Relationships.* New York: Harper & Row Publishers. A careful analysis of how women allow anger to defeat them. Lerner suggests ways that anger might be used and understood as a starting point to change instead of blaming others. She realistically states that the patterns in which we operate have served us well in some ways but can be changed slowly and intentionally to serve us better.

____1993. *The Dance of Deception—Pretending and Truth-Telling in Women's Lives*. New York: HarperCollins Publishers. In an age of political spin and defining words as common as "is", this book should be helpful to all of us! Whether we call it lying, or deception, or pretending, or denying, it is not "truth" and, as Lerner says, we are only as truthful to other people as we are to ourselves. This is a helpful beginning to understanding how skilled we can be at deception and how we might begin to change.

LESTER, Andrew D. 1995. *Hope in Pastoral Care and Counseling*. Louisville, Kentucky: Westminster John Knox Press. Hope is an essential ingredient in our religious experience. But many people exist in dysfunctional and despairing situations and cannot grasp the hope intended in deep faith. Lester analyzes these aspects of the human condition and sets forth methods by which a pastoral counselor or pastor could assist others in finding hope and wholeness.

McCLENDON, James Wm. Jr. 1995. *Making Gospel Sense to a Troubled Church*. Cleveland, Ohio: The Pilgrim Press. Rev. McClendon was called out of retirement to a church that was dying. In this book he presents some of the sermons he preached during his first year with that church. Each sermon is placed in the context of what was going on in that church. In the introduction to each sermon he explains what he believed the church should do and why. The book is full of theological reasoning and realistic ideas for making change even when change is resisted or even when it is welcomed.

McCULLOUGH, Donald W. 1995. *The Trivialization of God: The Dangerous Illusion of a Manageable Diety*. Colorado Springs, Colorado: NavPress. If we presume to know all about God and presume to define God by human terms we have made God trivial. This author uses biblical imagery and traditional stories (the golden calf and the prodigal son) convincingly showing readers that these stories are applicable to current issues as powerfully as they addressed the issues of biblical times. He challenges us to experience and worship God who is Most Holy.

MAY, Gerald G. 1988. *Addiction & Grace*. San Francisco: Harper and Row, Publishers. From his perspective as a psychiatrist, Dr. May studies the spiritual connections involved in psychology and the physiology of addiction. The latter is generally caused by a desire to keep control of our lives and the author explores the "theological and spiritual qualities of grace" as the alternative to addictive behaviors.

MELTON, J. Gordon, editor. 1986. *Enclycopedia Handbook of Cults in America.* New York/London: Garland Publishing Co. This handbook includes a section of clear, concise information on Satanism and the Church of Satan.

MICHALOWSKI, Kazimierz. DZIEWANOWKSI, Andrzej, photographer. 1968. *Palmyra.* New York: Praeger Publishers. Pictures and reports of anthropological digs and studies of ancient Palmyra of Syria.

MURRAY, Dick. 1987. *Teaching the Bible to Adults and Youth.* Creative Leadership Series. Lyle E. Schaller, Ed. Nashville: Abingdon Press. This is a helpful resource describing a wide range of methods that can be used to teach the Bible to these age groups. The last two sections are directed specifically to preachers and Christian education directors. This book includes an annotated bibliography for additional resources.

NEW YORK STATE POLICE Report, Edward VanderWall, Col. Deputy Superintendent Administrator, New York State Police Division Headquarters, Albany, New York. (Chad Campbell murder investigation from August 1, 1990)

NOLAN, Albert. 1988 (First Edition 1976) *Jesus Before Christianity.* Maryknoll, New York: Orbis Books. Nolan presents a view of Jesus, not as the object of faith, but as a historical person located in a particular situation. He says clearly that faith in Jesus is the intended outcome of this study, especially a renewed understanding about how we as individuals or as the church can address human suffering. He offers a perspective that was unique at the first writing and more relevant to biblical studies ten years later with this second edition. Good material for a Bible Study.

NORRIS, Kathleen. 1993. *Dakota: A Spiritual Geography*. New York: The Berkeley Publishing Group. Poetry and essays describe how the author was challenged to find peace and fulfillment in the often-desolate, windy, sandy, lonely, barren land of South Dakota. The people of her book are real and warm, and the space becomes holy space in Norris' telling. The chapter on *The Holy Use of Gossip* is a wonderful new way to view a troublesome characteristic of many church communities. The specific description of desolation in Norris' living space is highly transferable to spiritual desolation of anyone's life.

_____1996. *The Cloister Walk*. New York: Riverhead Books. This is a journal entry-style presentation of the year Ms. Norris spent involved with a monastic community. It is well-written but not as riveting as her earlier book.

_____1997. *The Psalms*. New York: Riverhead Books. The book is mainly a presentation of The Psalms but it includes an extensive Preface written in her conversational style that explains why she has come to treasure the Psalms and why she wanted to publish this edition. She presents good background information about the Psalms and about the importance of reading them as poetry and metaphor rather than literally.

PAGELS, Elaine. 1995. *The Origin of Satan*. New York: Random House. This book is primarily a study of the Satan portrayed in the New Testament gospels, but Pagels must begin at the beginning. She shows how the character of Satan evolved through ancient Near Eastern myths and the apocalyptic prophets during the time of the Exile to the Satan who was the intimate enemy of the newly developing Christian Church. This is a readable academic study that uses sound biblical exegesis and significant academic resources to support her theses.

_____ 1981. *The Gnostic Gospels*. New York: Random House. Pagels has done significant editing of the archeological discoveries in 1945 of "a collection of Gnostic Christian texts at Nag Hammadi in Egypt and has written this analysis of those discoveries. Her work is extensive and reads easily and understandably and should be included in the useful resources of lay people.

PASSANTINO, Bob and Gretchen. 1995. *Satanism*. Grand Rapids, Michigan: Zondervan Publishing House. This booklet is part of a series published by this company called *Guide to Cults and Religious Movements.* The authors of this booklet actually interviewed Anton Szandor LaVey, founder of the Church of Satan, on August 5, 1994—one of few interviews he has given. The booklet gives specific information about Satanism, i.e., classification into six different levels; discusses common rumors about Satanism; states the Satanic Creed as published by the Church of Satan; gives misconceptions of Satanic holidays and discuses criminal activity often associated with Satanism.

PECK, M. Scott. 1997. *People of the Lie: The Hope for Healing Human Evil.* Simon & Shuster. (Also available in Audio Cassette under the title: *People of the Lie: Possession & Group Evil*) One of several books from a popular writer and speaker. This particular book examines the phenomenon of denial and blame in relationships and communities and how he believes they relate to evil in our communities and between one another.

PERKINS, Pheme. 1988 (First Edition 1978). *Reading the New Testament.* New York: Paulist Press. Written especially for young people, this is a very easily followed "one-volume introduction to the New Testament." It includes outlines of every book of the New Testament, recent historical and archeological information and new maps. Study questions and activities are included at the end of each chapter as well as questions for personal reflection. Good Bible Study resource.

PERRIN, Norman and DULING, Dennis C. 1982. *The New Testament: An Introduction. Proclamation and Parenesis, Myth and History.* Second Edition. San Diego: Harcourt Brace Jovanovich, Publishers. This was the main text for a seminary class on the New Testament. It contains a great deal of information about the world at the time of the New Testament and about the people who were the focus of the writings and the developing Christian church. The appendices add supplementary information about what it meant to be religious in New Testament times, background on the canon of the entire Bible, some significant archeological findings, and a collection of prayers and sayings from several Greco-Roman sources. The bibliography is significant and supplementary readings are suggested at the end of each chapter. A valuable resource!

PETERS, Ted. "Satanism: Bunk or Blasphemy." *Theology Today.* Vol. 51, No. 3, October 1994. Dr. Peters, professor of systematic theology at Pacific Lutheran Seminary and Graduate Theological Union in Berkeley, California, writes a careful analysis of Satanism, including what it is to various people and how different groups in society respond to Satanism. He discusses several levels of Satanism and describes the groups who might dismiss it all as "bunk". Then he analyzes the topic as "purposeful blasphemy," suggesting that Satanism is dangerous because it makes society careless about the way we use words about God's work. He says, "talking about God orders our soul. To blaspheme God destroys our soul." He contends that the main intent of Satanism is to blaspheme God and Christianity.

PHILLIPS, J.B. 1961. *Your God is Too Small.* New York: The MacMillan Company. This book is dated in its style but contains relevant reflection on the various images human beings develop about God, the nature of sin and how it is experienced, and the role of Jesus as the Christ. Still a good little book for a small group discussion and study.

POLING, James. 1991. *The Abuse of Power: A Theological Problem.* Nashville: Abingdon Press. Relying a good deal on his experiences of working with survivors of sexual abuse as well as the perpetrators, Dr. Poling examines a very current issue for clergy and other church leaders. All too often problems are dismissed as personal or private when they are significant examples of power abuse and issues the church must begin to address directly. He believes in a God whose power can be seen in the hope and beauty that grows out of ambiguity—circumstances that seem overwhelmed with evil. He calls the church and the leaders to respond and move for change.

ROBINSON, James M., ed. 1978 *The Nag Hammadi Library*. San Francisco: Harper and Row. This one volume contains all the documents "of the secret Gnostic writings of ancient Egypt" believed to have been buried around 400 A.D., discovered in 1945, and only released ten years before this printing. Included with the English translations of the ancient texts are commentaries by the editors and translators. A fascinating read for anyone "interested in Egypt, archaeology, the Bible, the evolution of Christianity and the story of Western civilization."

RUPP, Sr. Joyce. 1985. *Fresh Bread*. Notre Dame, Indiana: Ave Maria Press. This is only one of Sr. Joyce's books on spiritual growth, but it is my favorite. It is a handbook for meditation for a year following the seasons with poetry, brief reflections and Bible verses for daily reading and prayer.

RUSSELL, Jeffery Burton. 1977. *The Devil: Perceptions of Evil from Antiquity to Primitive Christianity*. Ithaca, New York: Cornell University Press. Dr. Burton claims that this is not a theological study but a historical search for understanding the personification of evil, or the Devil. This volume examines ancient myths, legends, art and literature only up to the early days of Christianity. He has written other volumes to pick up the study. This is easily read even though a very scholarly examination. It is theological because of the topic and cannot help challenging our personal understandings of evil and the role of the Devil in today's world.

SAKHEIM, David K. and Susan E. Devine 1992. *Out of Darkness: Exploring Satanism and Ritual Abuse.* New York: Lexington Books (An Imprint of Macmillan, Inc.). (Paperback: 1997) A collection of reports by forensic psychiatrists, theologians, an FBI agent and two survivors of ritual abuse. All of the reports give a picture of satanic cults in the early 1990's.

STANFORD, Peter. 1996. *The Devil: A Biography.* New York: Henry Holt and Company. This is an easily read presentation of historical and cultural backgrounds of our current concept of the Devil. He presents a good background to the idea of Satanism, which began mostly in England and Europe. He discusses in detail the book *Michelle Remembers*, one of the first stories to surface in the 1980's of satanic ritual abuse.

STENDAHL, Krister. 1976. *Paul Among Jews and Gentiles.* Philadelphia: Fortress Press. This somewhat controversial collection of essays by a well-known scholar suggests new understandings of the traditional teachings of Paul's writings in the New Testament. "Paul must be heard as one who speaks of his call rather than conversion, of justification rather than forgiveness, of weakness rather than sin, of love rather than integrity, and in unique rather than universal language." This would be a good Bible Study book with challenges to common understandings of Paul and early Christianity.

TERRIEN, Samuel. 1983. *The Elusive Presence: The Heart of Biblical Theology.* San Francisco: Harper & Row, Publishers. The understanding of "covenant" has traditionally been described as the major concept in understanding our relationship to God. But this author presents a powerful argument that experiences of God's presence and absence are even more important when we seek to know God. A very academic exegisis of these experiences, this book provides excellent material for sermon preparation and for Bible Study. Extensive end notes as well as an index of both Bible references and authors will help in using this as a resource.

TROSKOSKY, Betty, ed. 1989. *Palmyra: A Bicentennial Celebration: 1789-1989.* Interlaken, New York: Heart of the Lakes Publishing Company. This book was compiled to celebrate the 200th anniversary of the founding of the town of Palmyra, New York, and contains much from a book written over 60 years earlier. It also includes photographs, drawings, and reports from many churches, service and fraternal organizations.

WANGERIN, Walter, Jr. 1984. *Ragman and Other Cries of Faith.* San Francisco: Harper & Row, Publishers. A collection of original and biblical stories told from the perspective of an inner-city pastor to relate Christian values and understanding in a new way.

WATSON, Lyall. 1995. *Dark Nature: A Natural History of Evil.* New York: HarperCollins Publishers, Inc. What is the source of Evil? What causes Evil? Watson approaches this timely question from a biological view and it is most helpful. He gives many examples to show that human beings are not the only life forms to show compassion—and also not the only life forms to experience or give expression to evil. He attends court trials for accused murders searching for evidence of evil in the eyes of those eventually convicted. But he is convinced, and gives convincing argument, that evil happens when we do not overcome evil with good, but most especially when we do not find appropriate balance in life itself. The invitation is to be intentional about choices that are made in all of life.

WATTS, Alan W. 1951. *The Wisdom of Insecurity: A Message for an Age of Anxiety.* New York: Random House (Vintage Books). Although this book is tiny and rather dated, its concepts continue to remind me of the necessity of what we call "letting go" today. I have never forgotten the image of being caught in the current of a river when the only hope for being safe is allowing the river itself to get you to shore—trying to fight the current or to control your direction is a sure way to exhaustion and defeat. It seems to be the way to get through *Chaos*.

WESTBERG, Granger E. 1997 (Thirty-fifth Anniversary Edition). *Good Grief.* Minneapolis: Fortress Press. A tiny book outlining ten stages of grief, this book states realistic and ordinary feelings and responses most people experience as they move through the grief process. The goal is to find hope and strength through the process. This book is encouraging in its authenticity of pain and sorrow on the way to new joy.

WESTERMANN, Claus. 1982 (First Edition in German 1978) *Elements of Old Testament Theology.* Atlanta: John Knox Publishers. This is a foundation book on the Old Testament which contains history as well as interpretation and understanding of the people of Old Testament times. Good discussions of God as well as concepts of judgment and compassion; also includes the connection of the Old Testament to the New Testament and the role of Jesus Christ.

WINK, Walter. 1980. *Transforming Bible Study.* Nashville: Abingdon Press. Combining use of imagination and feeling with a search for the original historical setting of various Bible verses, Dr. Wink gives a variety of approaches and questions for students of the Bible. Includes plenty of material for several sessions using the specific questions he has included. A great resource for expanding a study based on his ideas and suggestions.

ORDER INFORMATION

Obtain **Crossroads Choices: Confronting Chaos** from
your bookstore. If your bookstore does not have it in stock,
you can order it directly for $16.95 plus $3.50 for shipping
and handling per book. If five or more copies are ordered,
send only $2.00 shipping and handling per book.
Colorado residents add 4.8% sales tax.

Please send _____ copies @ $16.95   _____
Colorado residents add 4.8% sales tax   _____
Shipping and handling @ $3.50 per book   _____
  ($2.00 per book for five or more)

                                  TOTAL   _____

(Please print or type information)

Name_____

Address_____

City_____State_____Zip_____

Phone (____)_____(if we need to contact you
                                      about this order)

Mail this order blank with check or money order payable to
Kekova Press at:

         Kekova Press, Publisher
         1900 E. Girard Place, #1005
         Englewood, CO 80110
         Phone: 303-762-0094
         Email: kekova@sni.net